NEAR DARK

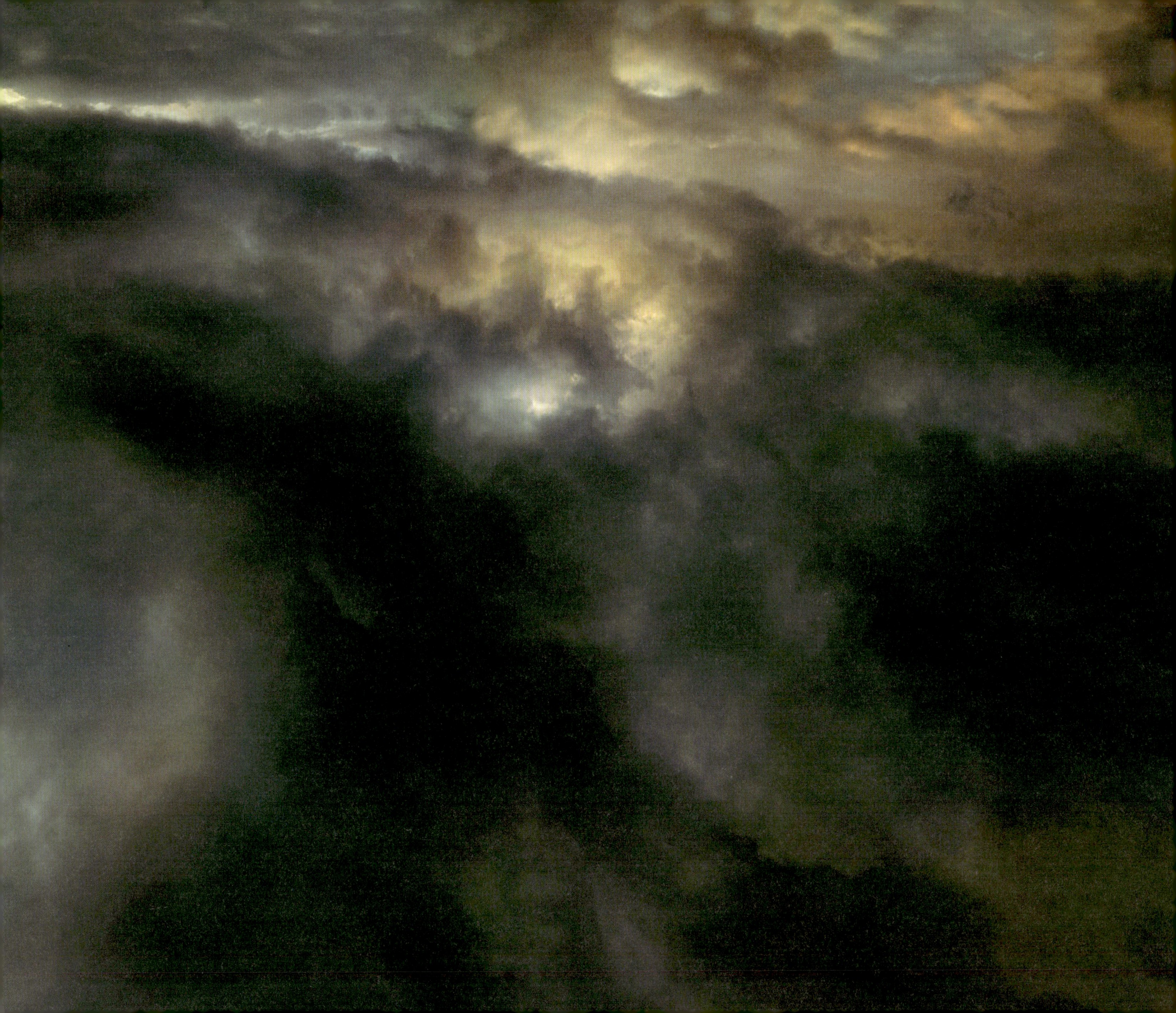

Chris Dorley-Brown

NEAR DARK

London Photographs 2009-2025

Dewi Lewis Publishing

NEAR DARK

Diane Smyth

Near Dark, the 1987 film by Kathryn Bigelow, starts out in the everyday. A young man meets a young woman and starts talking to her. But somehow the scenes are suffused with a sense of unease, the feeling that all is not well, a foreboding that makes the viewer watch closely. Soon the reason becomes clear, and the foreboding shifts into something more concrete. The young woman is a vampire, and before long she has bitten the man.

Horror films often start out this way, and it's often where they're most unsettling. The sense of impending doom makes every detail seem suspect and throws every character under suspicion, creating a hyper vigilance that feels like anxiety. In *Near Dark* it's the man who initially seems threatening, over-confident and harassing an unenthusiastic woman; she's gentle and pale and seems too fey to fend off an attack, though there's little to suggest one's coming. It's just an unsettling atmosphere, the part of the horror film that makes the everyday strange.

There's something of this apprehension in Chris Dorley-Brown's photographs, which are also titled *Near Dark* – a name which, he says, has literal and metaphorical meanings. Many of the images were shot at twilight, the darkening sky signalling a shift in mood, but they were taken in his hometown, London, between 2009 and 2025. It's hard to say exactly what makes them feel ominous. It could be his large-format camera, which puts everything into forensic detail, or the often-distanced view. It could be the empty streets because, especially post-Covid, empty streets often read as peculiar. But, as at the start of a horror film, there's nothing that's obviously threatening.

Dorley-Brown was inspired by *Near Dark*, as well as films such as George A. Romero's *Dawn of the Dead* (1978) or Val Guest's *The Day the Earth Caught Fire* (1961), both of which deal with disaster. He was also thinking of post-apocalyptic video games and grime music, the latter invented in London and drawing on bleak soundscapes and lyrics. JMW Turner was on his mind too, another Londoner whose images conjure visions of doom. Painting in the first half of the 19th century, Turner showed fires, storms, and war; his swirling skies record the effects of pollution, whether caused by the industrial revolution or an exploding volcano.

Dorley-Brown's inspirations draw on a kind of sublime, they're dystopian fantasies which evoke a thrilling sense of dread. They flirt with the idea of the wild, the uncontained, or the unknown, with the idea that there are aspects of life beyond human control or even comprehension. "Whatever is fitted in any sort to excite the ideas of pain, and danger, that is to say, whatever is in any sort terrible, or is analogous to terror, is a source of the sublime; that is, it is productive of the strongest emotion which the mind is capable of feeling," wrote Edmund Burke in the 1750s.

But though Dorley-Brown's images evoke unease, they don't directly reveal their source. Like the first ten minutes of a horror film, they don't show the monster – at least not in an obvious way. In fact they don't show anything in particular. Instead he works with something much more pervasive, scenes from everyday London which deliberately avoid famous sights or easily identifiable dates. He's working with the familiar, with views that, if you live in the city, you've usually long stopped noticing. By presenting them in photographs, in particularly detailed images, he makes you look again.

It feels close to defamiliarisation, the technique of presenting the familiar in a strange way so it can be seen anew. Russian formalist Viktor Shklovsky proposed this was the purpose of art in a 1917 essay, 'Art as Technique', writing that "art removes objects from the automatism of perception" and illustrating what he meant with two examples from Tolstoy – one describing flogging in distant terms, the other from a horse's point of view, bewildered and bewildering. In their crystal-clear vision of London, Dorley-Brown's images do something similar. If there's an alien here it's behind the camera not in front, giving an alien-eye view.

Shklovsky doesn't say so, but it's probably inevitable that defamiliarisation is unsettling. Like the sublime, or like the first ten minutes of a horror film, defamiliarisation suggests the world can be unknown or unknowable, that we could be wrong-footed by the ordinary, or not at home in our hometown. In fact, by making us look again, Dorley-Brown makes us question how well we know these streets; some of his images include layers of history, for example, showing how quickly the city is evolving. In many of his photographs gleaming skyscrapers rise up in the distance, like the covers of 70s sci-fi novels. Other images show building sites, or cranes, or demolitions.

Actually London is constantly changing. It's one of the most expensive cities in the world and the grimy corners Dorley-Brown photographs are often taken over by developers, not always for everyone's good. Dorley-Brown says his images capture the breakdown of the post-war social contract. One of his shots shows the Robin Hood Gardens social housing estate being knocked down, for example, while others depict blocks of flats covered in graffiti. There's a photograph of a building in Hackney Wick, with huge writing that reads "Shithouse to penthouse", a comment on gentrification.

But if developers sometimes ride roughshod over locals, 'progress' also fails other needs. Dorley-Brown's images show roads and railways, which, though they're now everyday, were also once new and shocking. In Turner's time steam trains seemed a terrible imposition on the environment; these days we all know that cars pollute, but somehow we still use them. In the future, an MOT Centre may look like a blot on the landscape, not an unremarkable London scene.

And perhaps too that's why the emptiness of Dorley-Brown's images seems ominous. One day the roads we take for granted may be devoid of cars or even people, driven out by environmental concerns or disasters. Dorley-Brown started making these photographs before Covid, but they prefigure just such an event. Pollution and global warming are spiralling out of control – quite literally, not just in the sense of the sublime.

In 1979 Ridley Scott made *Alien*, a scary film that, famously, leaves nearly everything to the viewers' imaginations. "You don't show the monster too many times because you'll get used to him and you never want to get used to him — ever," he has said. "That's always been my thesis. The best screening room in the world is the space between your ears, which is your brain. So, it's learning to tap into the human brain to show just so much. Let the brain do a lot of the work. That's where you start to tap into people's anxieties."

The best horror films are never about the monsters. *Dawn of the Dead* is a parable about consumerism; *Near Dark* plays into fears about being hunted, its hero a cowboy who farms cattle on land taken from native Americans. Though they're presenting fictions, these films create something documentary, something about contemporary fears. They show the anxieties that are in viewers' brains. And though Chris Dorley-Brown sticks to the humdrum, he manages to do something similar, revealing a dystopia we're usually too jaded to see. His photographs play with anxieties but, as Covid showed, these are anxieties that are well-founded. In fact perhaps they are realities, and perhaps the real monsters are us.

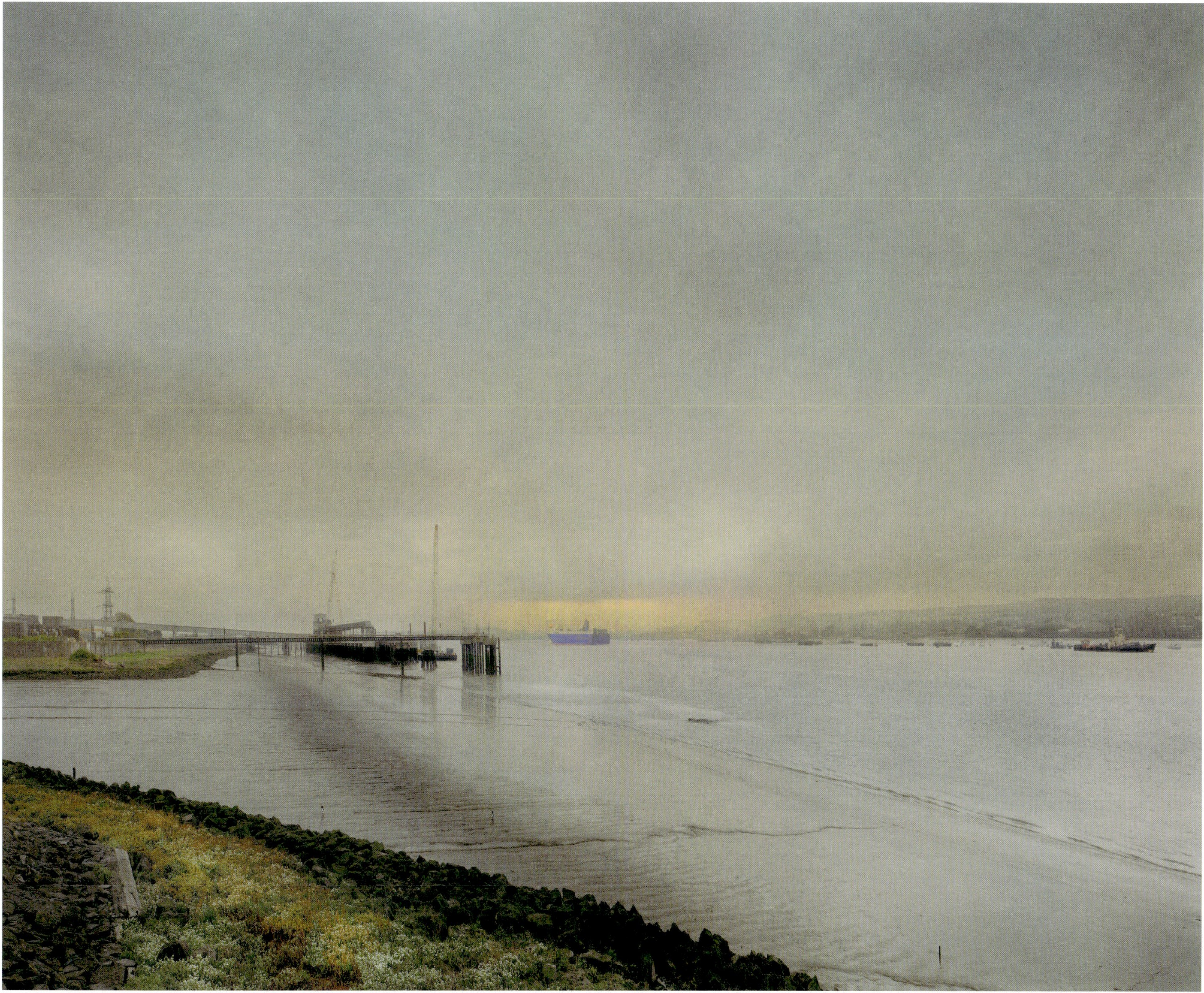

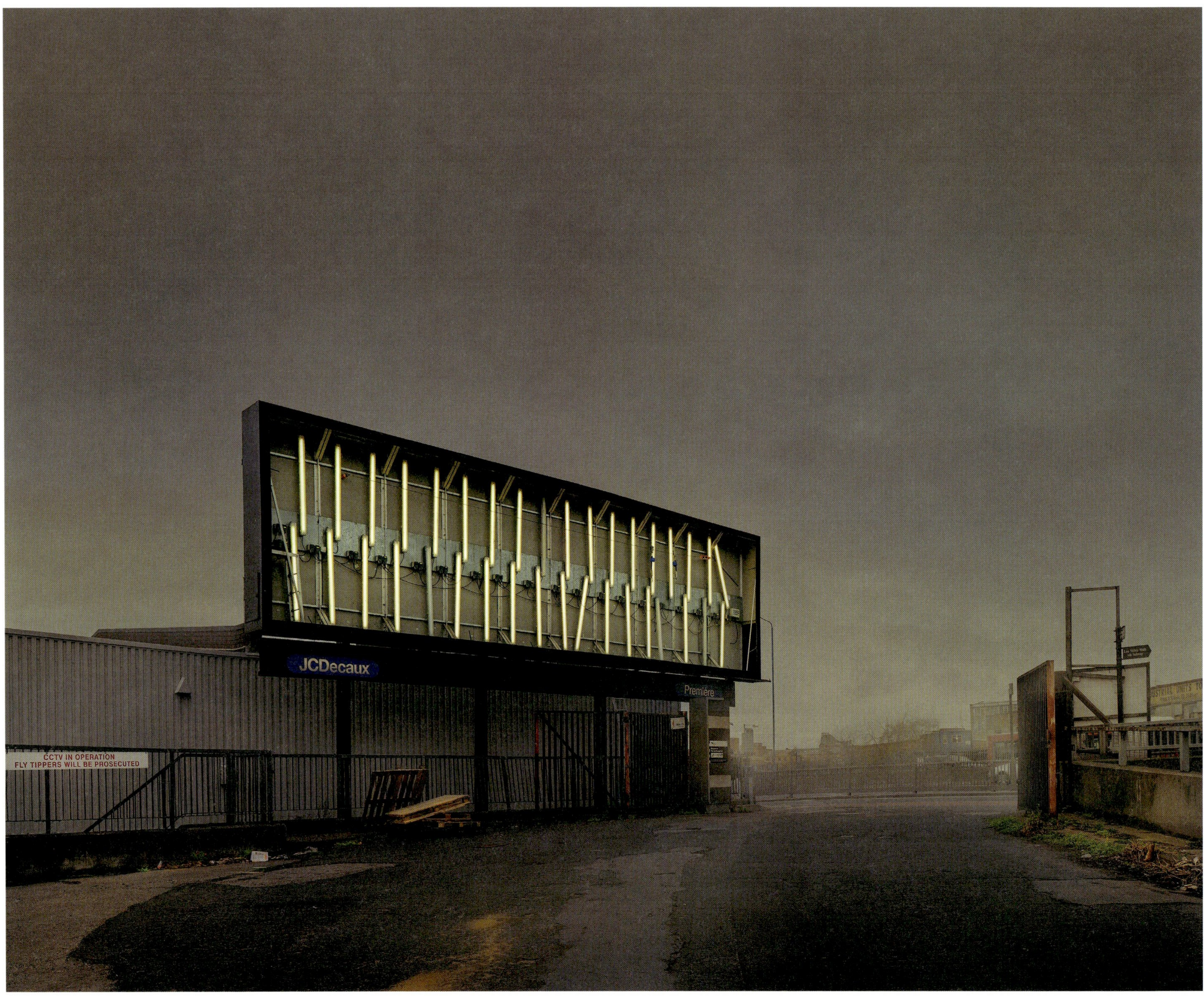
JCDecaux
Première
CCTV IN OPERATION
FLY TIPPERS WILL BE PROSECUTED

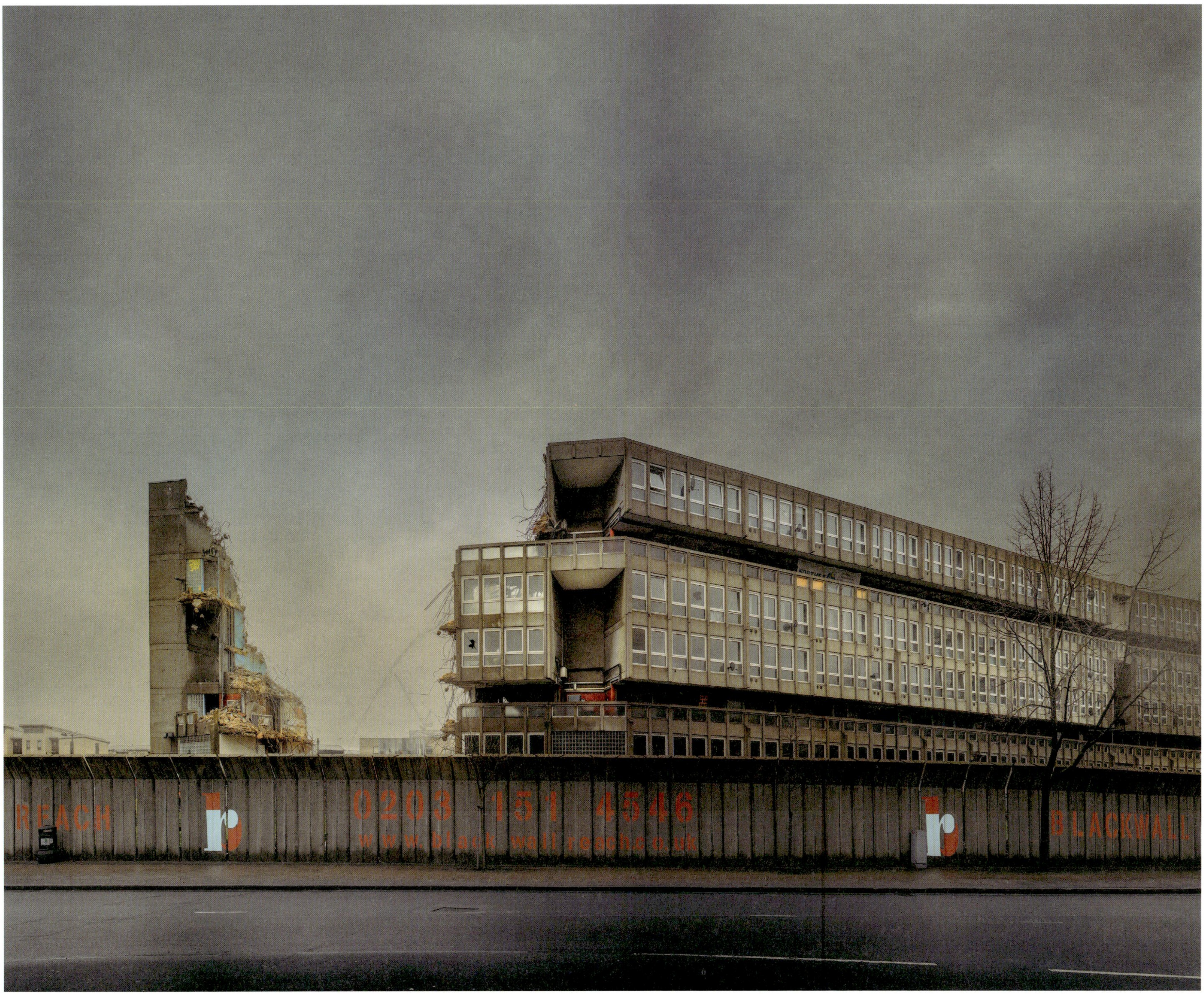
REACH
0203 151 4546
www.blackwallreach.co.uk
BLACKWALL

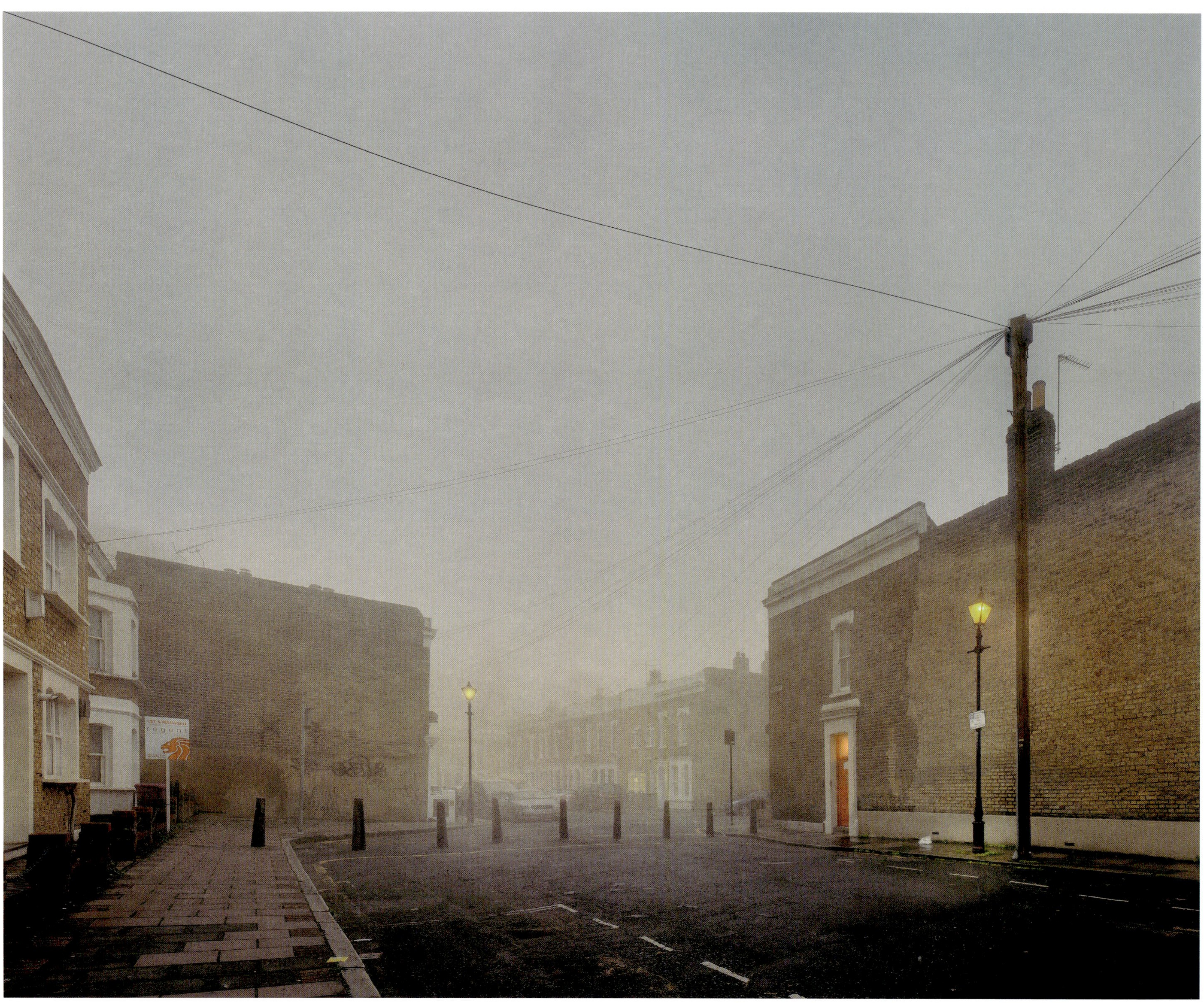
LET & MANAGED
regent

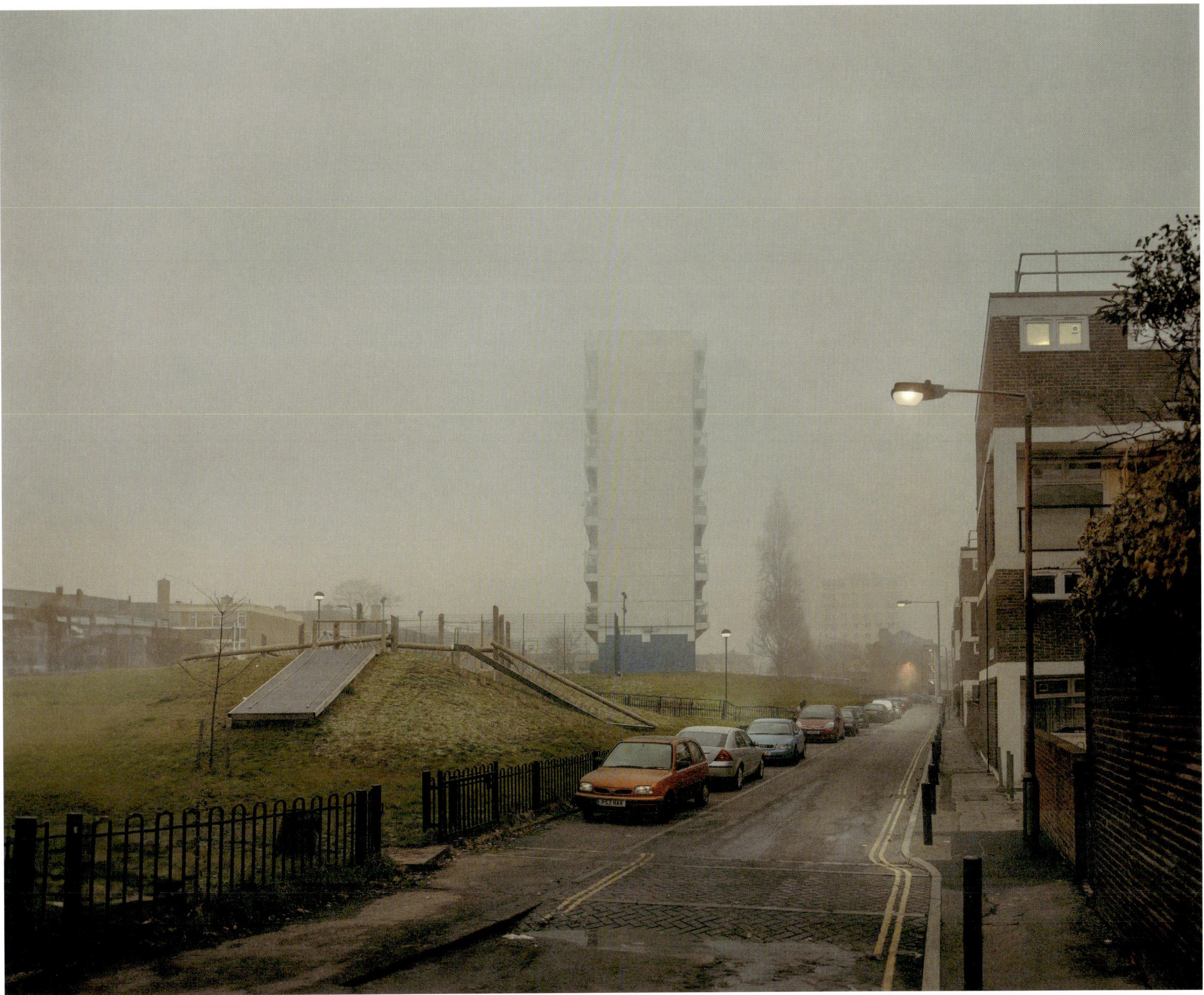

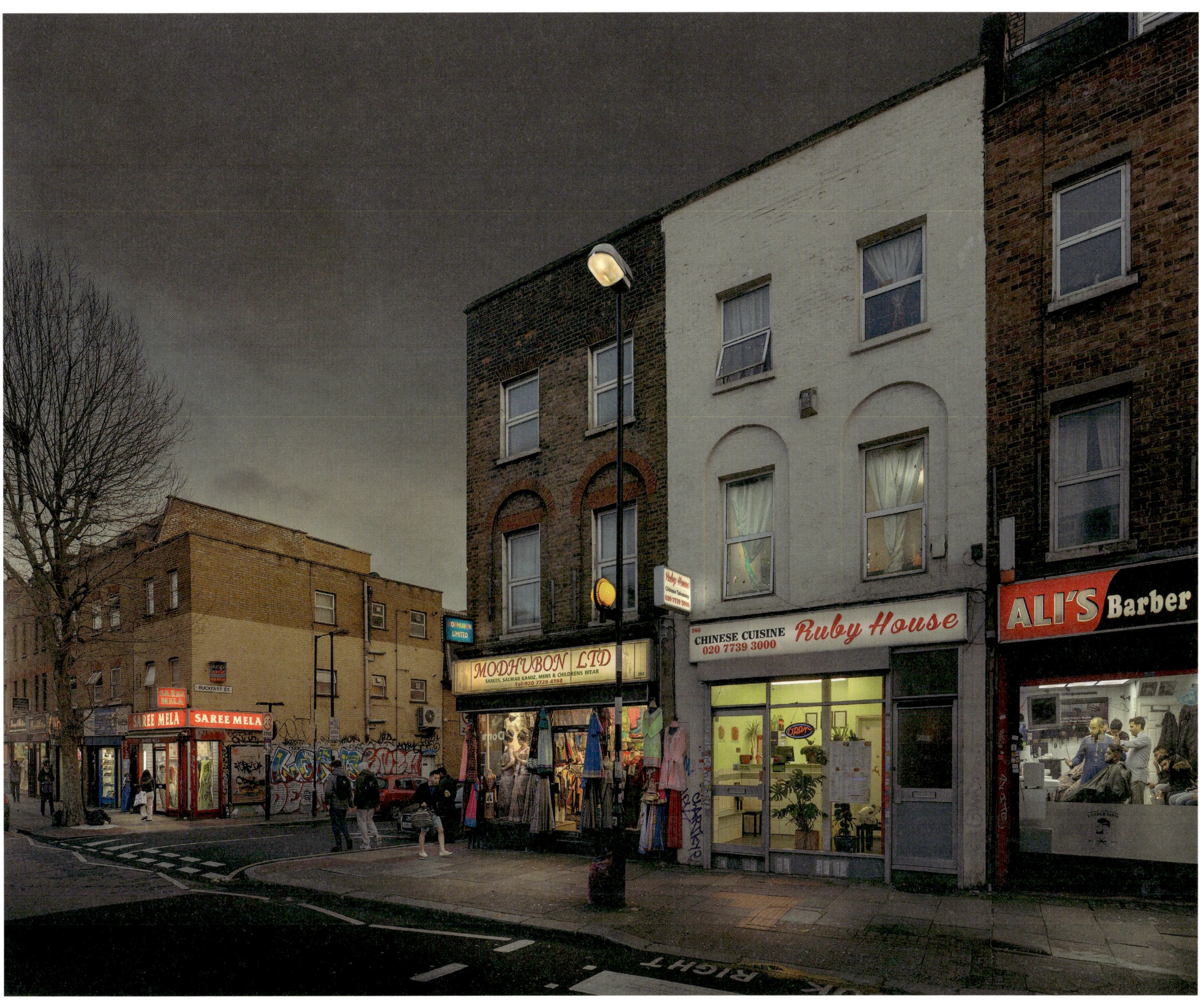

MODHUBON LTD
SAREES, SALWAR KAMIZ, MENS & CHILDRENS WEAR
CHINESE CUISINE
020 7739 3000
Ruby House
ALI'S Barber
SAREE MELA
SAREE MELA

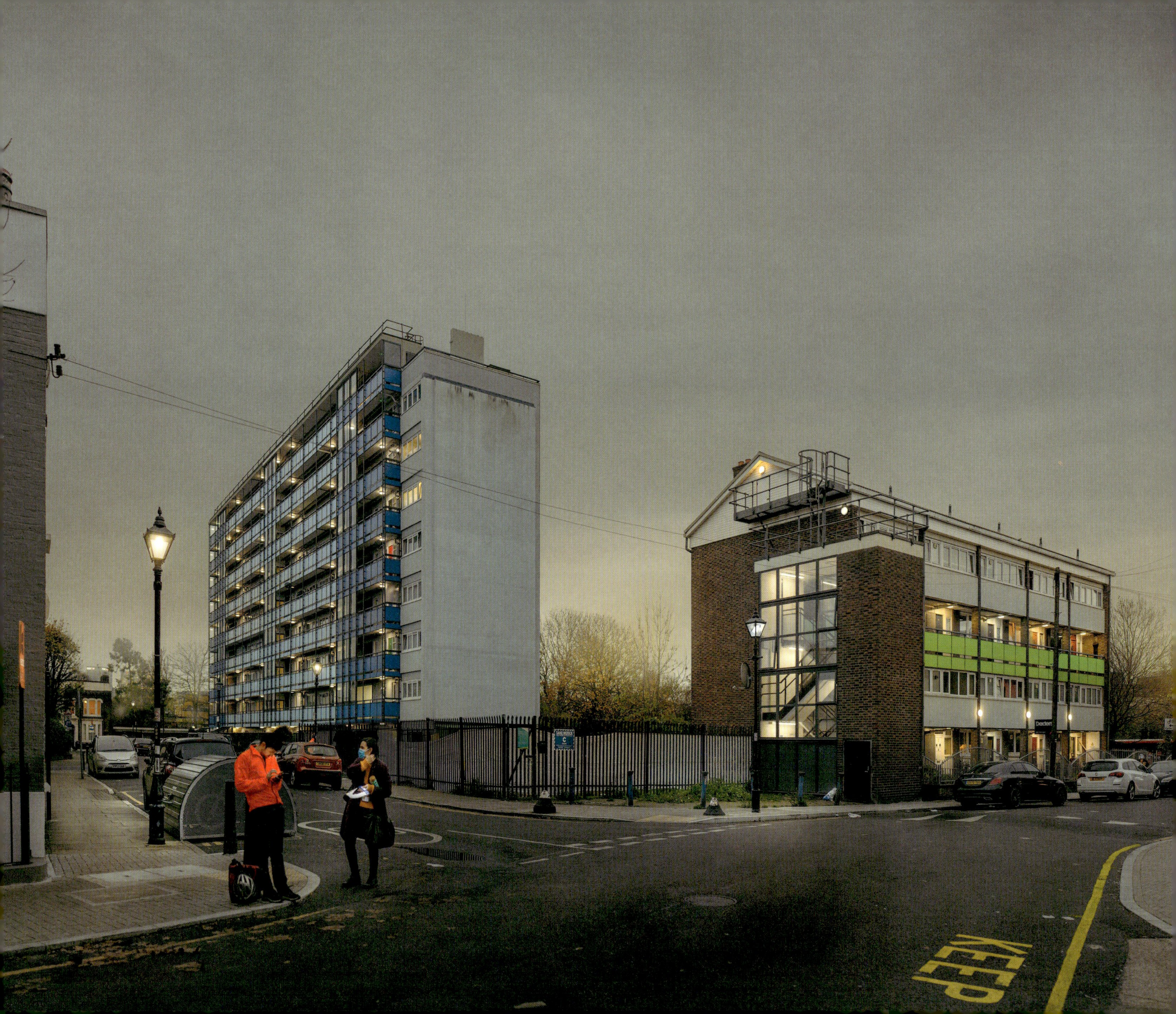
KEEP

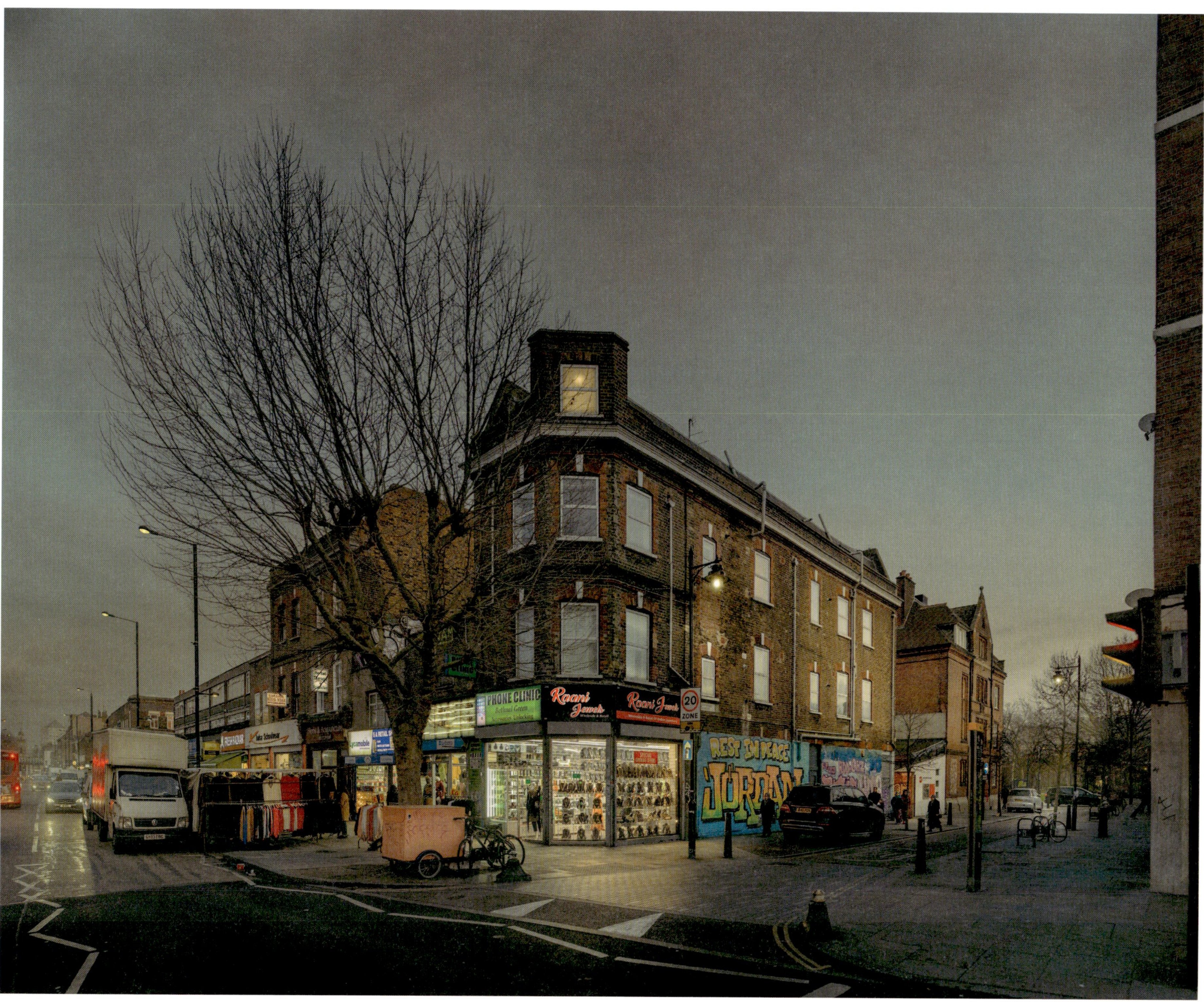
PHONE CLINIC
Bethnal Green
Raani Jewels
Raani Jewels
20
ZONE
REST IN PEACE

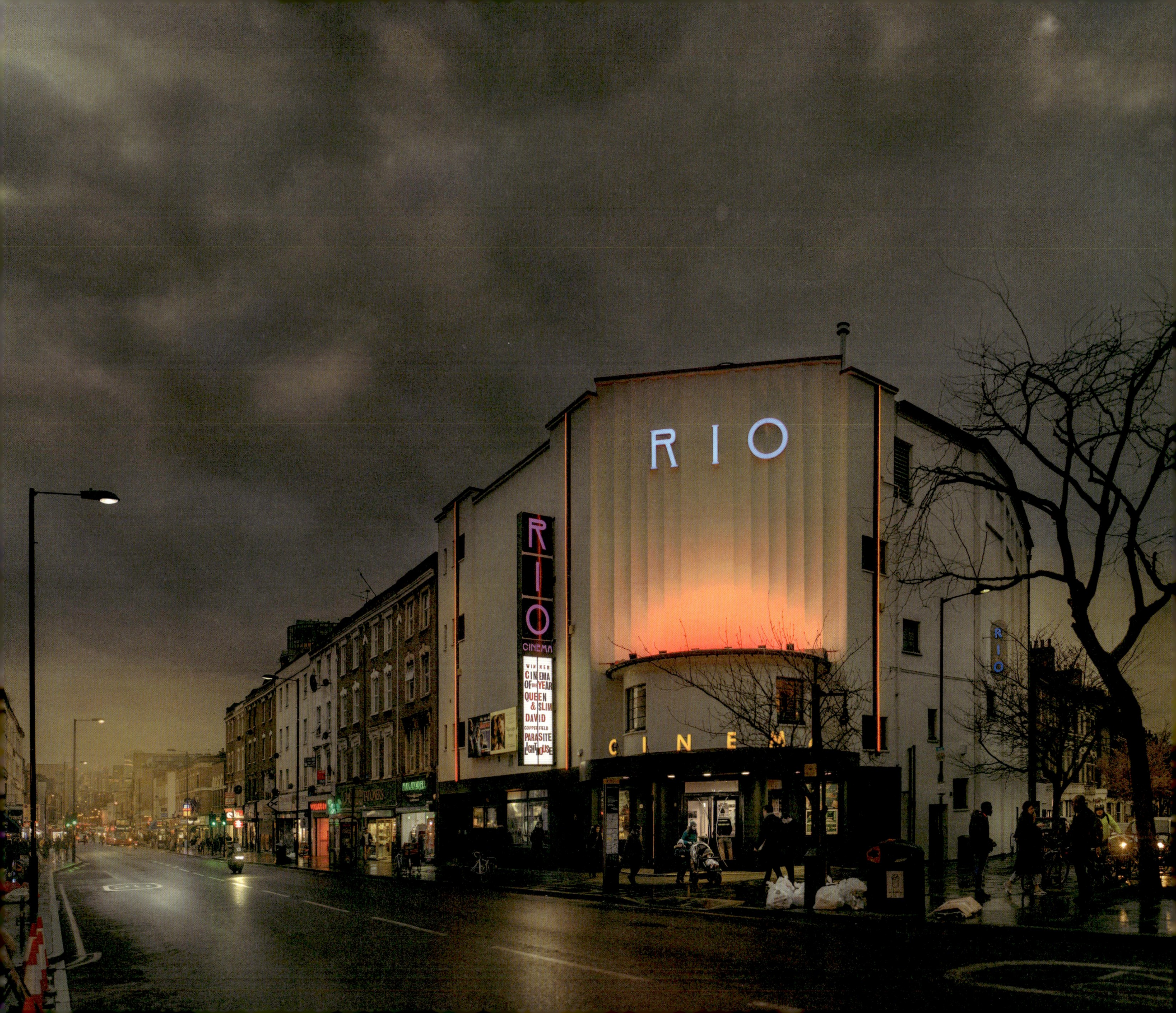
RIO
RIO
CINEMA
WINNER
CINEMA
OF THE YEAR
QUEEN
& SLIM
DAVID
COPPERFIELD
PARASITE
LIGHTHOUSE
CINEMA
RIO

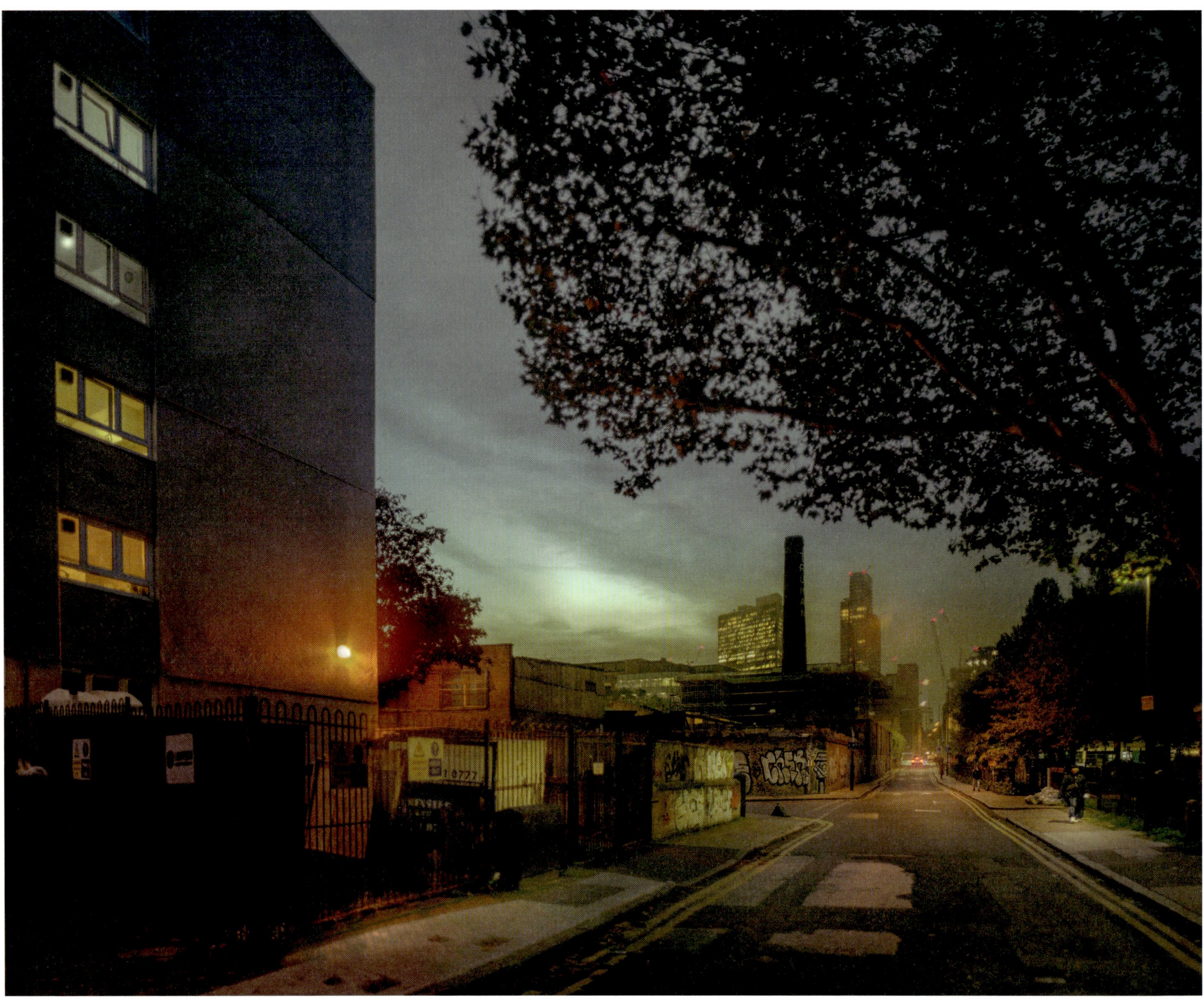

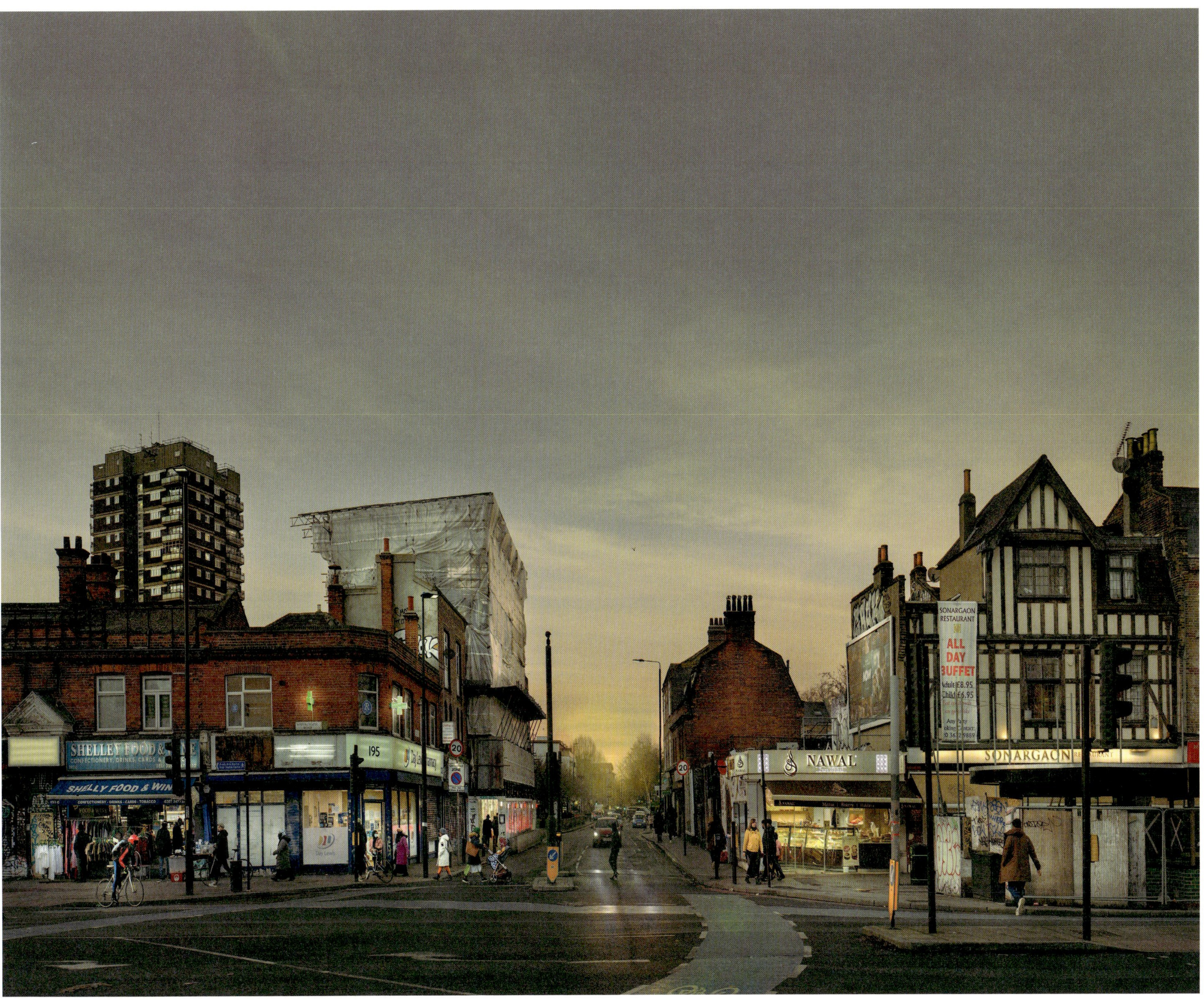

195
20
NAWAL
SONARGAON
RESTAURANT
ALL
DAY
BUFFET
Adult £8.95
Child £6.95

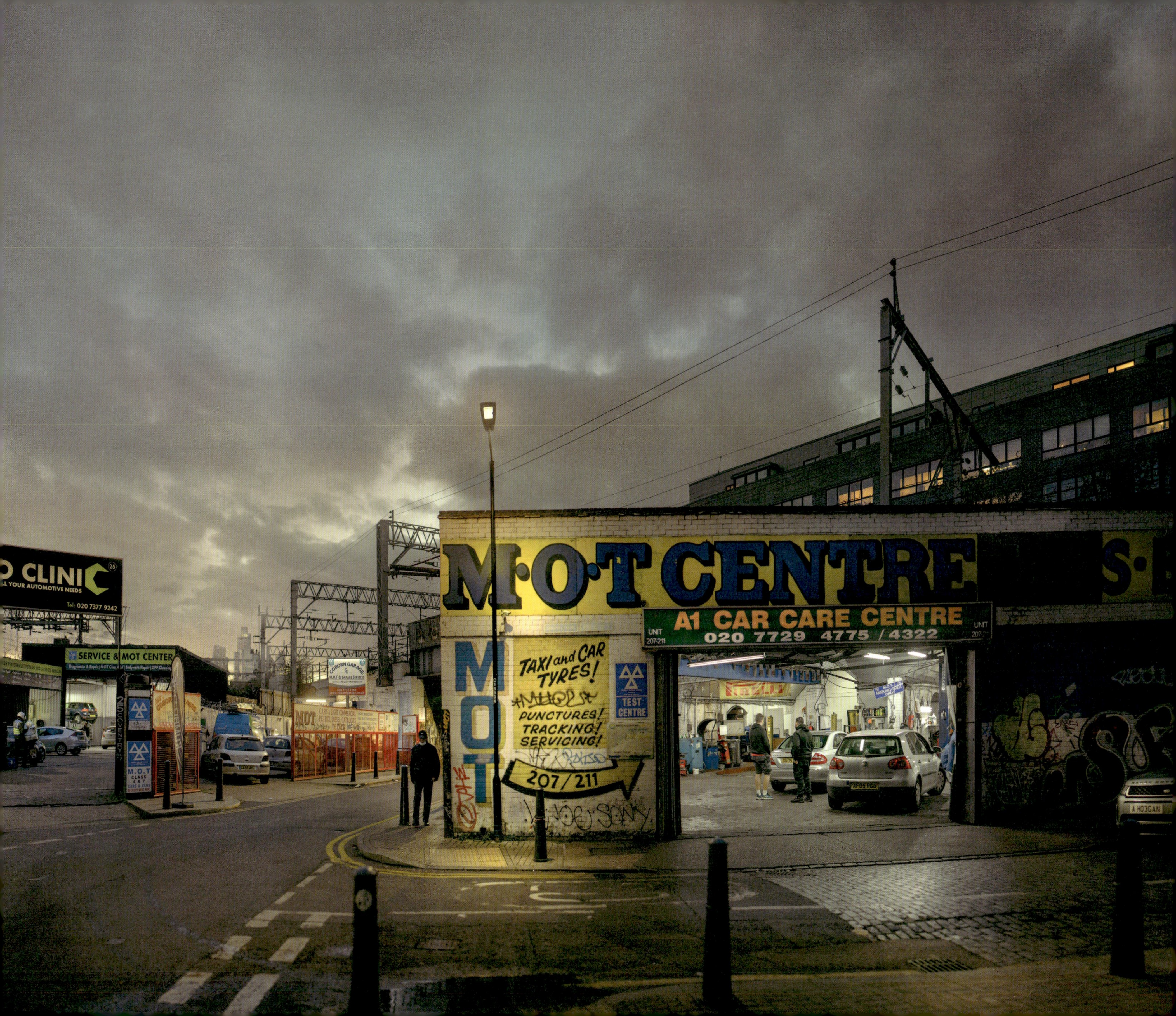
M·O·T CENTRE
A1 CAR CARE CENTRE
UNIT 207-211
020 7729 4775 / 4322
MOT
TAXI and CAR TYRES!
PUNCTURES!
TRACKING!
SERVICING!
207/211
TEST CENTRE
SERVICE & MOT CENTER
Tel: 020 7377 9242

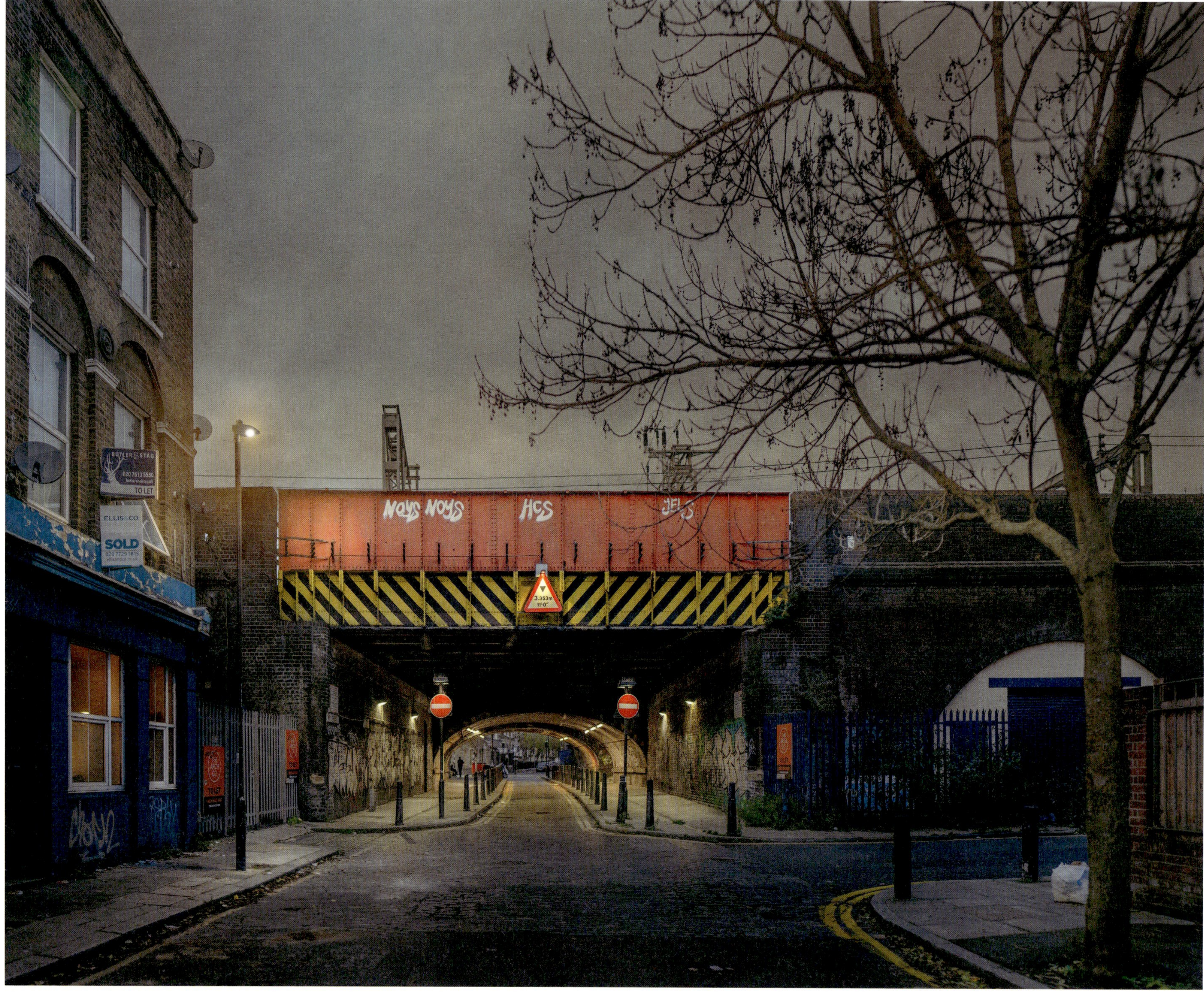

TO LET
ELLIS&CO
SOLD
3.353m
11'0"

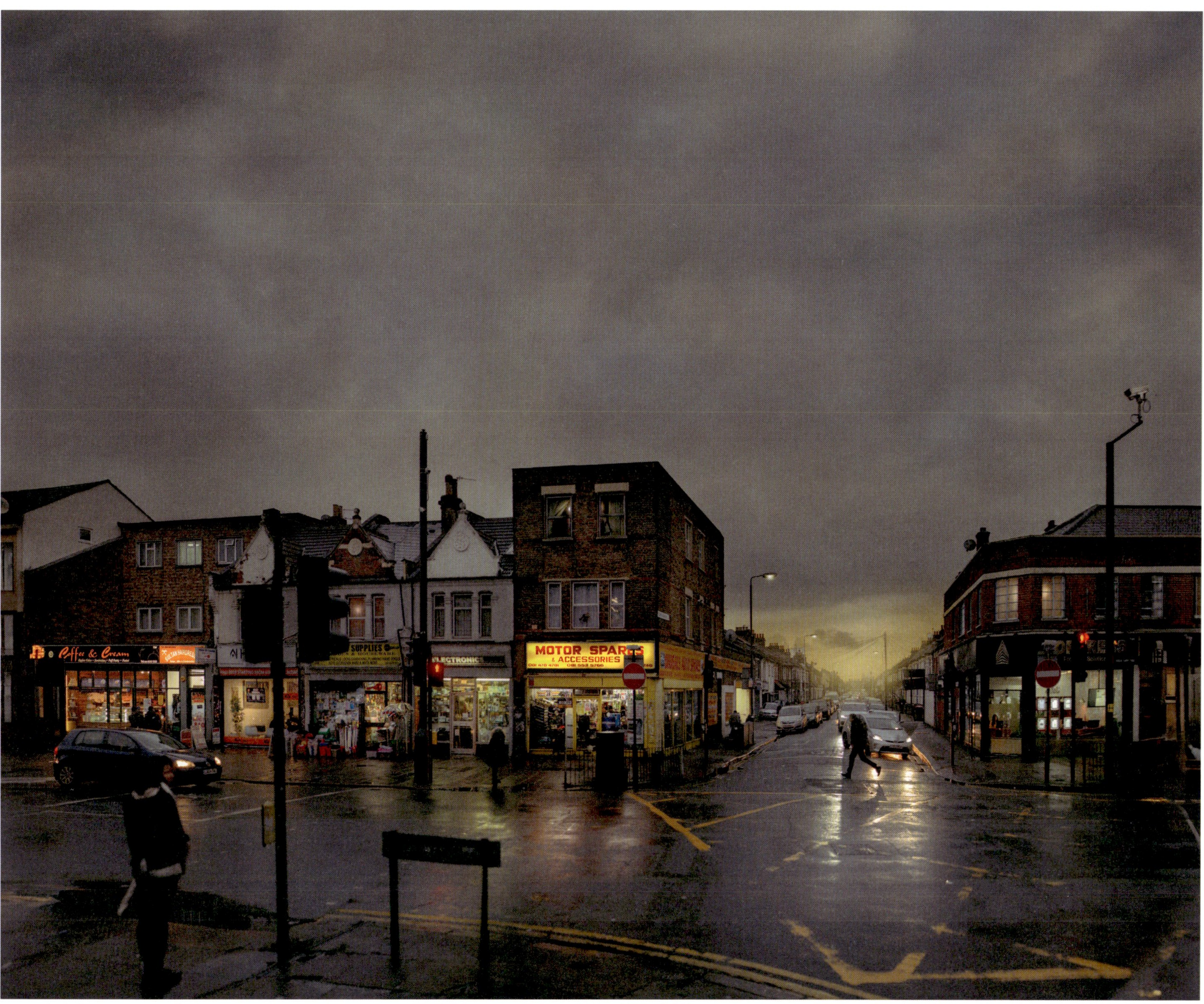
Coffee & Cream
SUPPLIES
& ACCESSORIES

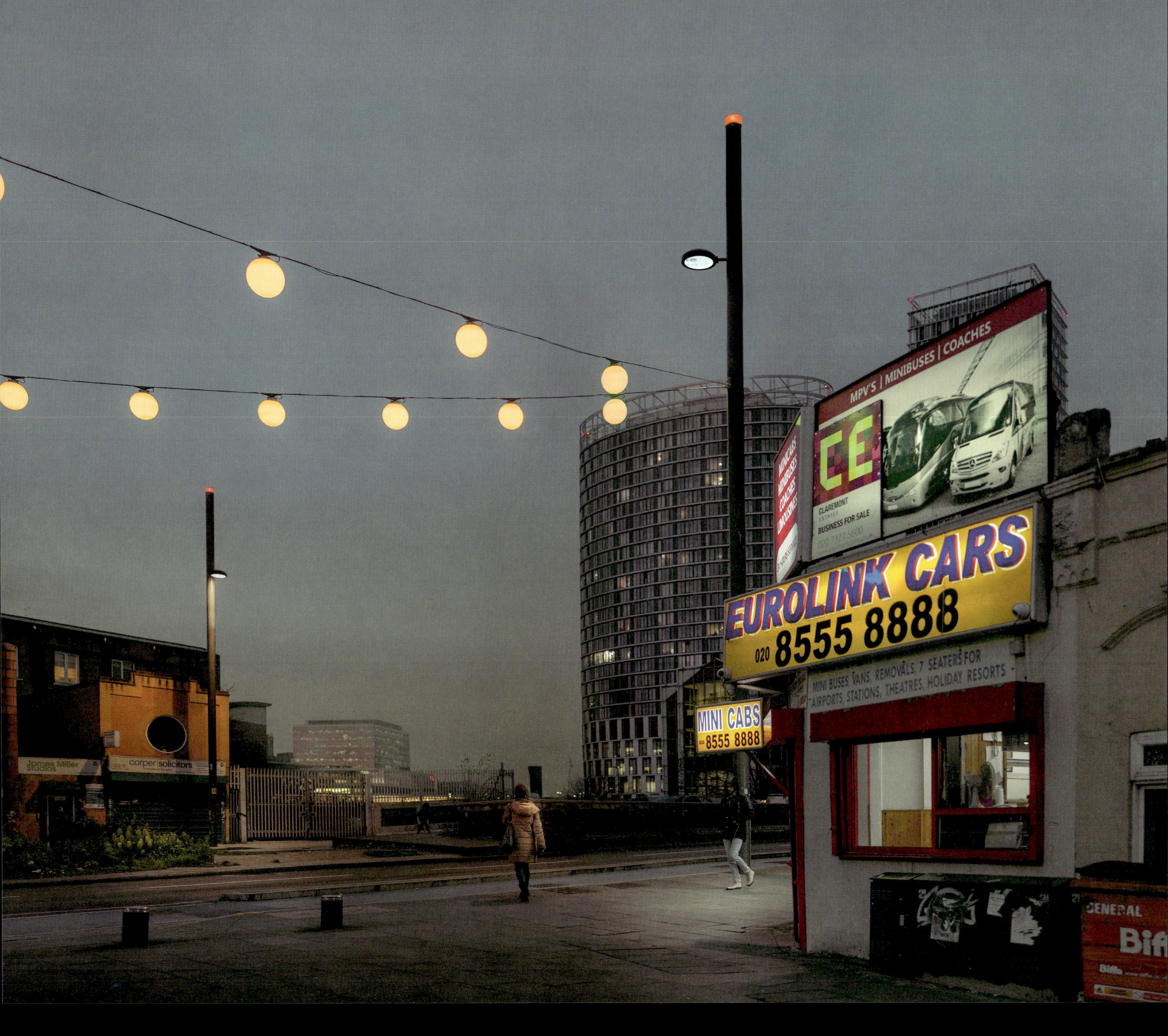

MPV'S | MINIBUSES | COACHES
CLAREMONT
BUSINESS FOR SALE
EUROLINK CARS
020 8555 8888
MINI BUSES, VANS, REMOVALS, 7 SEATERS FOR
AIRPORTS, STATIONS, THEATRES, HOLIDAY RESORTS
MINI CABS
020 8555 8888
James Miller Studios
corper | solicitors
GENERAL

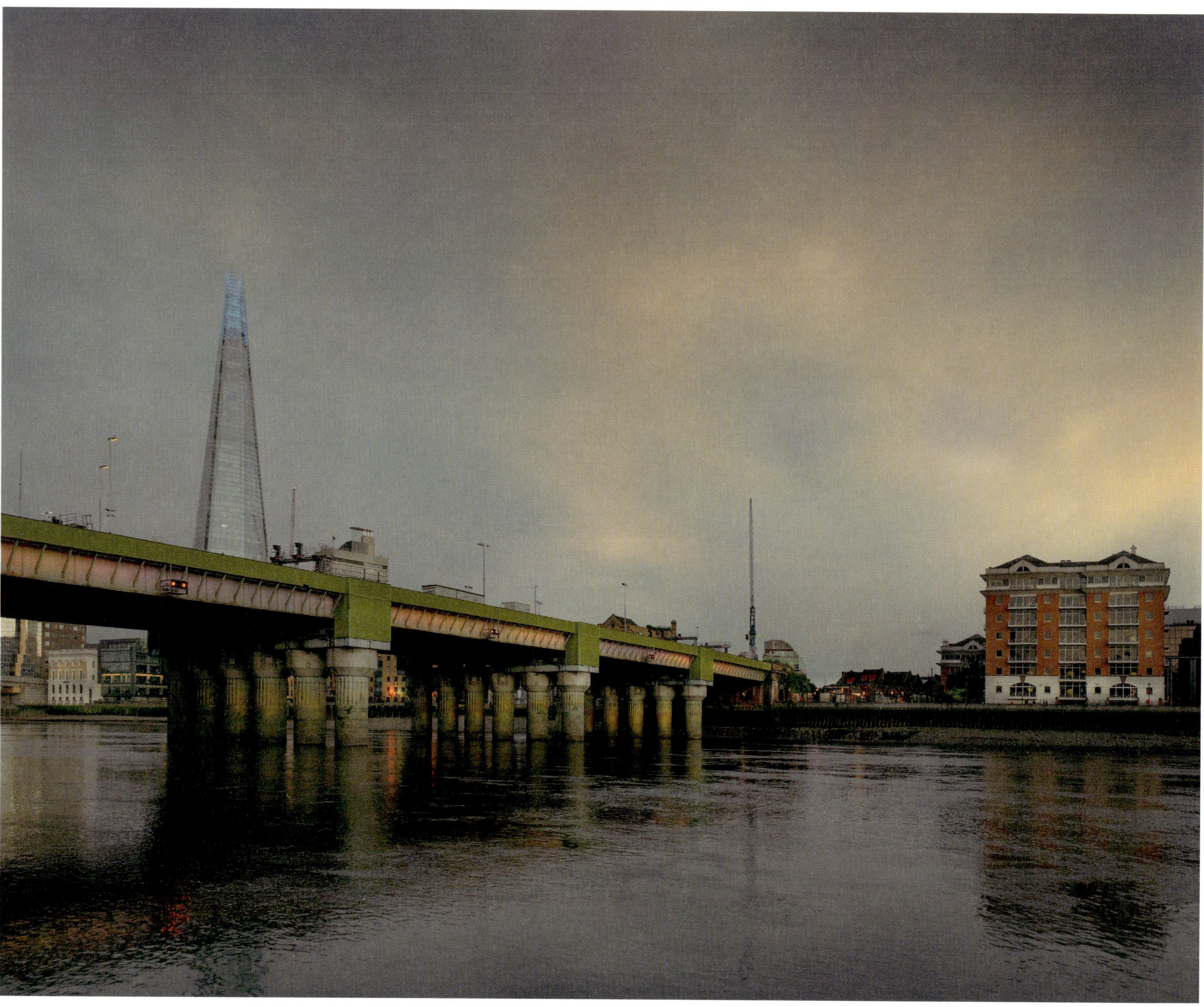

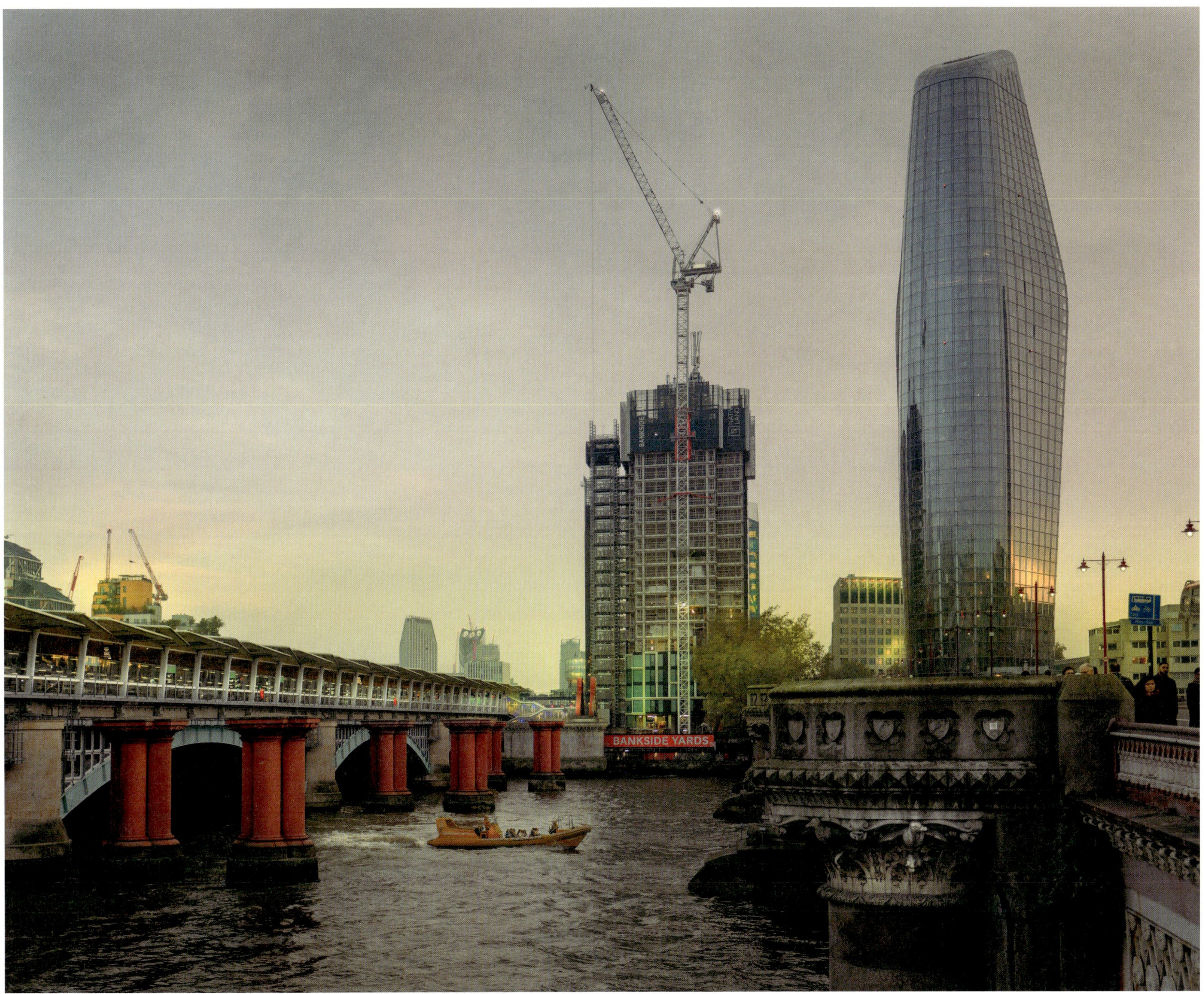
BANKSIDE YARDS

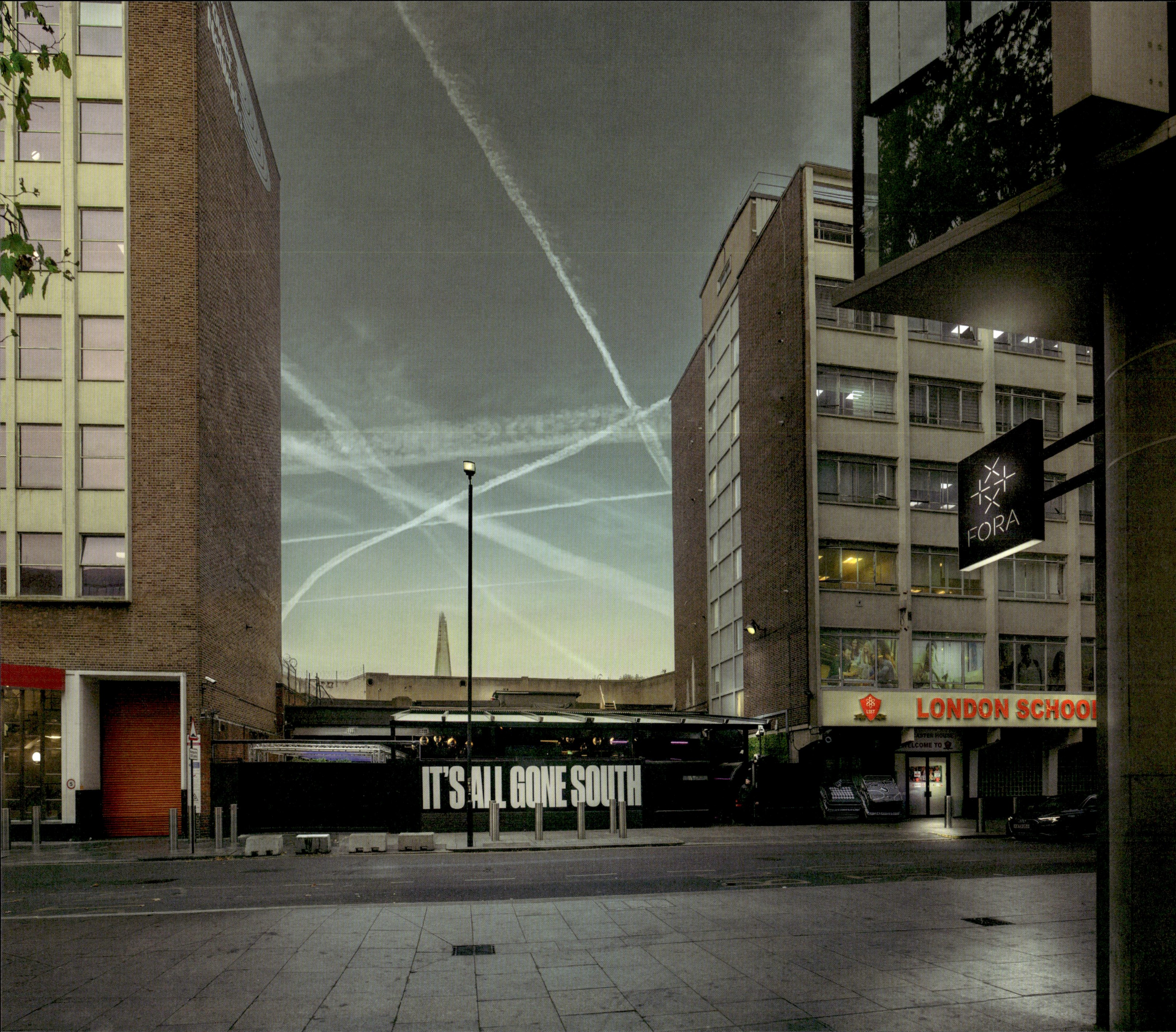
IT'S ALL GONE SOUTH
FORA
LONDON SCHOO

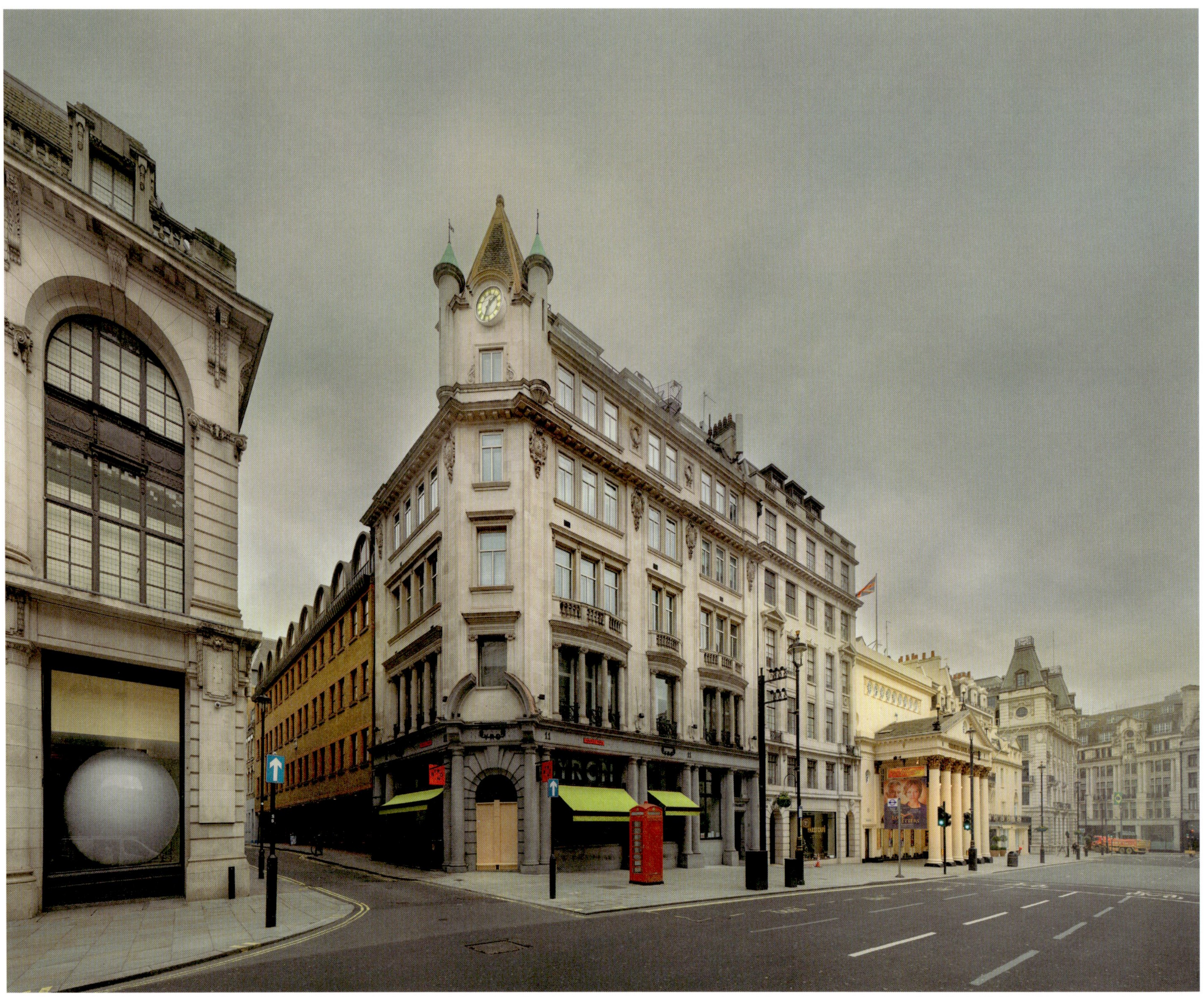

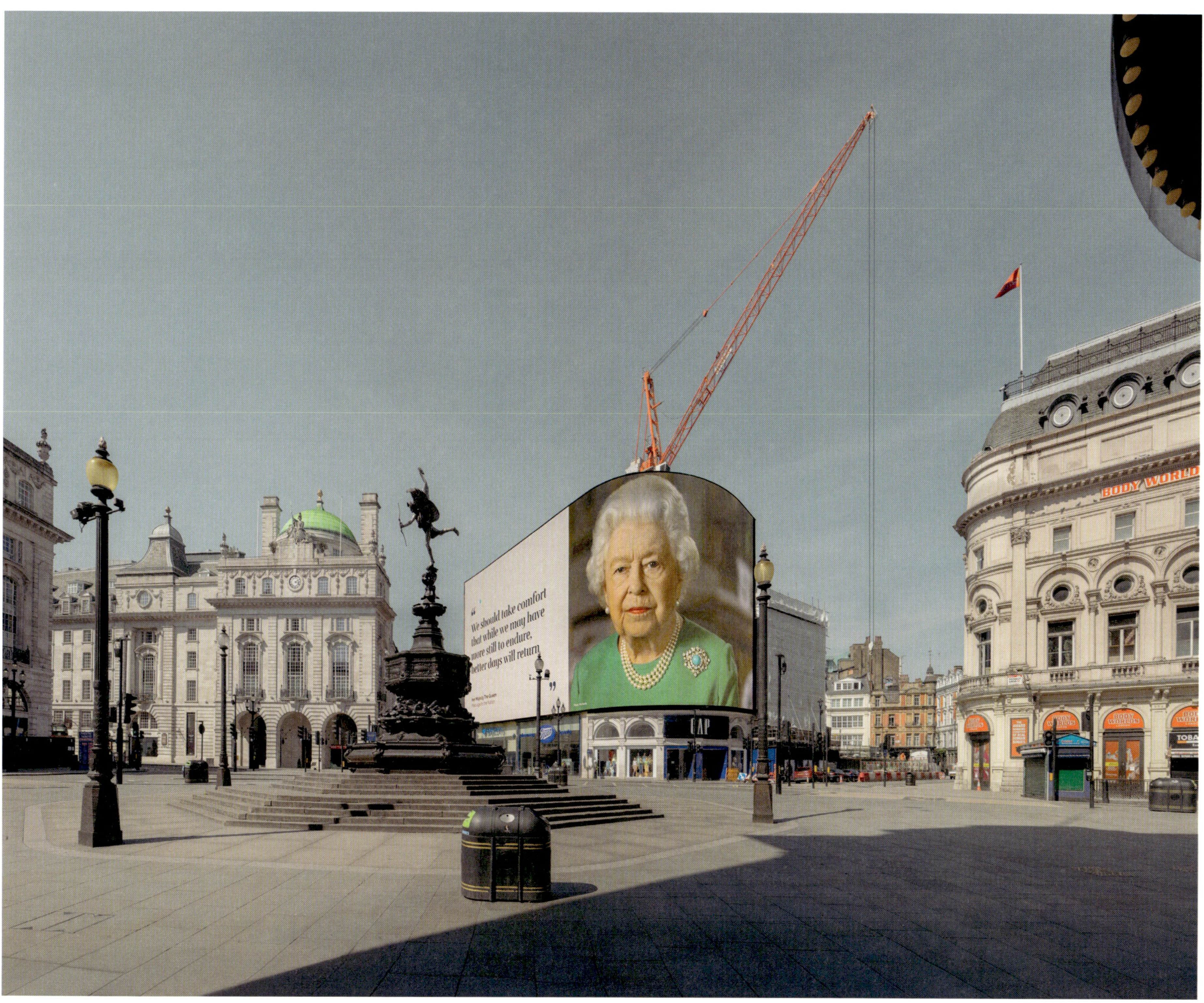

“We should take comfort
that while we may have
more still to endure,
better days will return”
GAP
BODY WORLDS

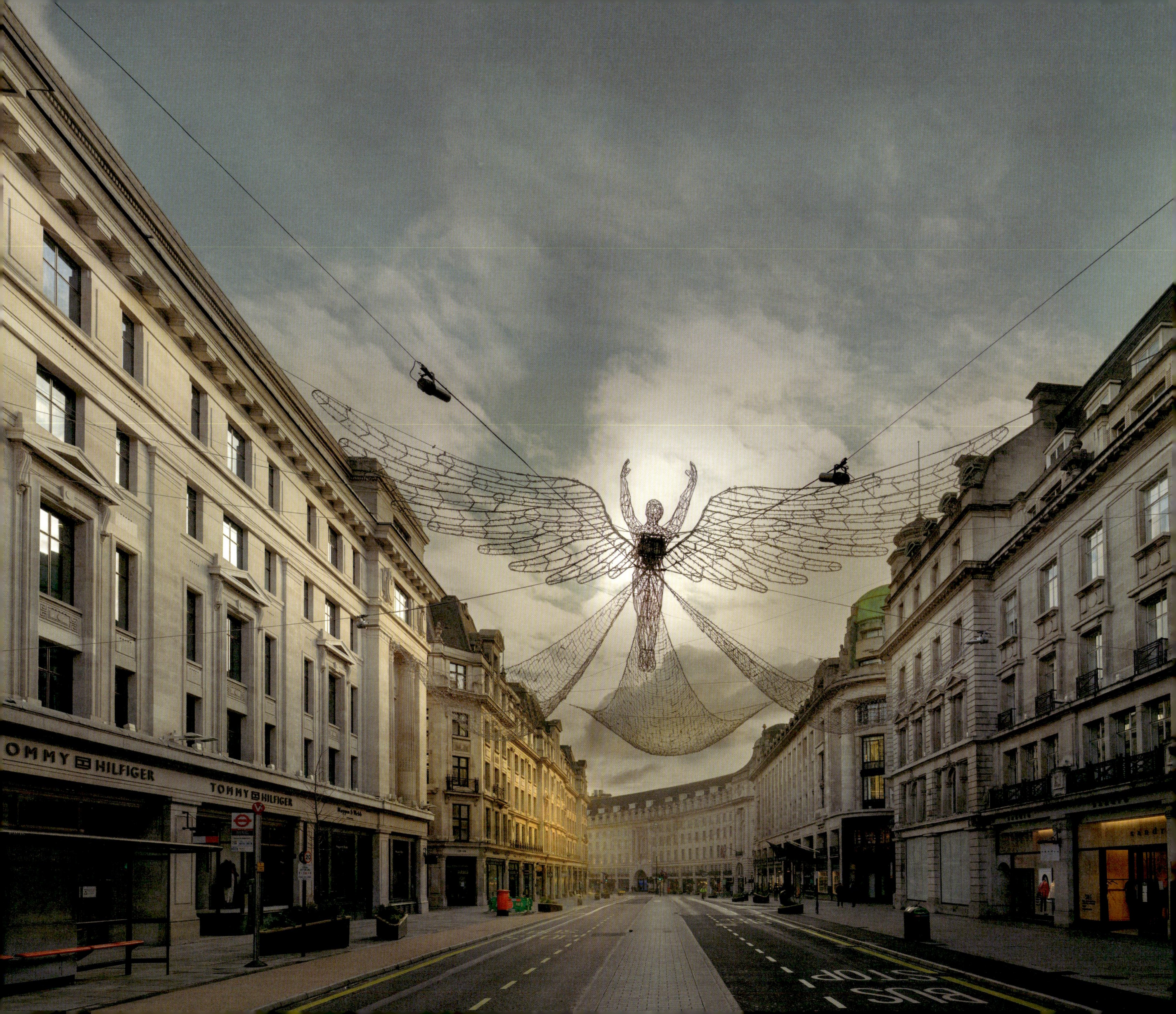
OMMY HILFIGER
TOMMY HILFIGER

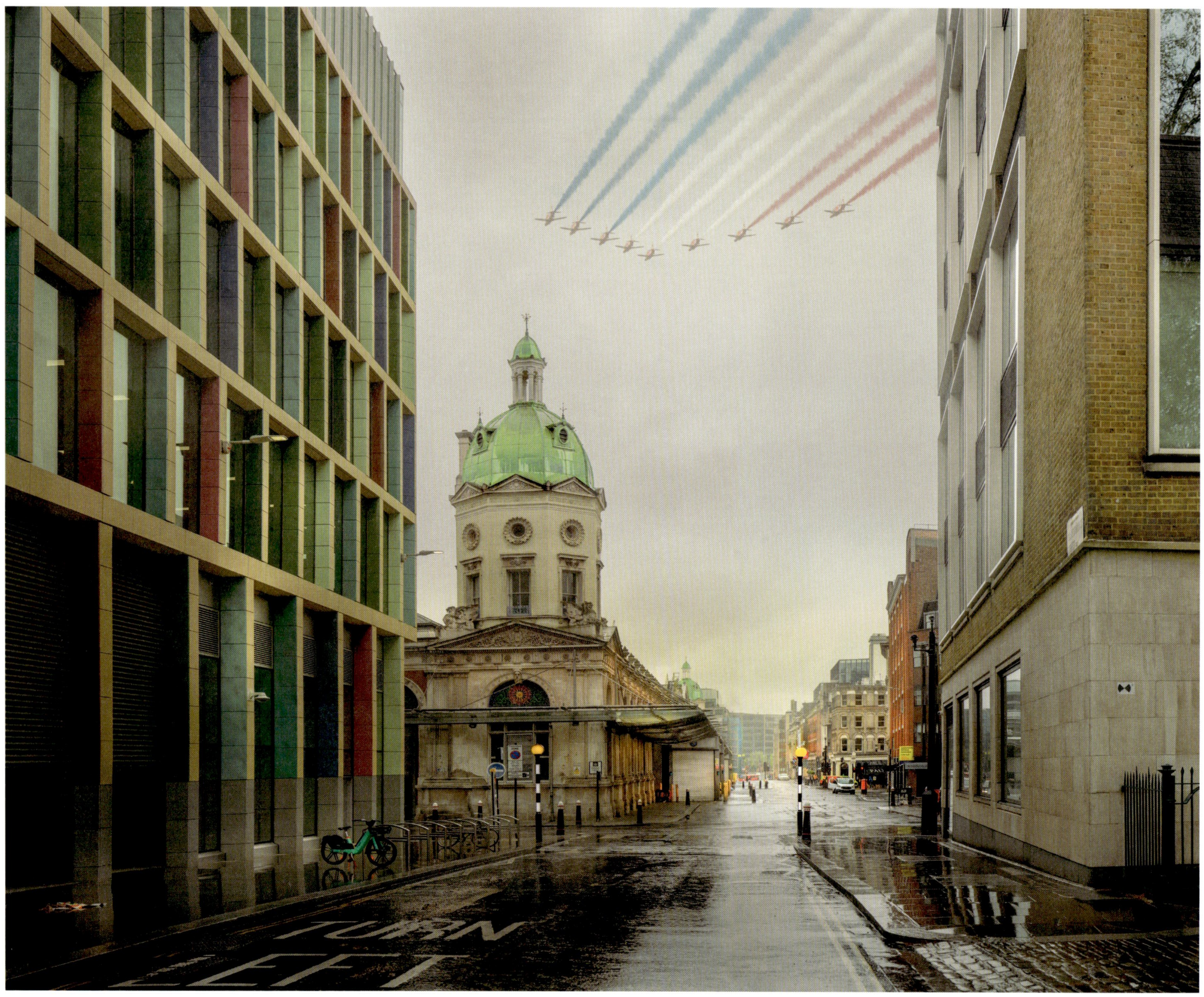
TURN

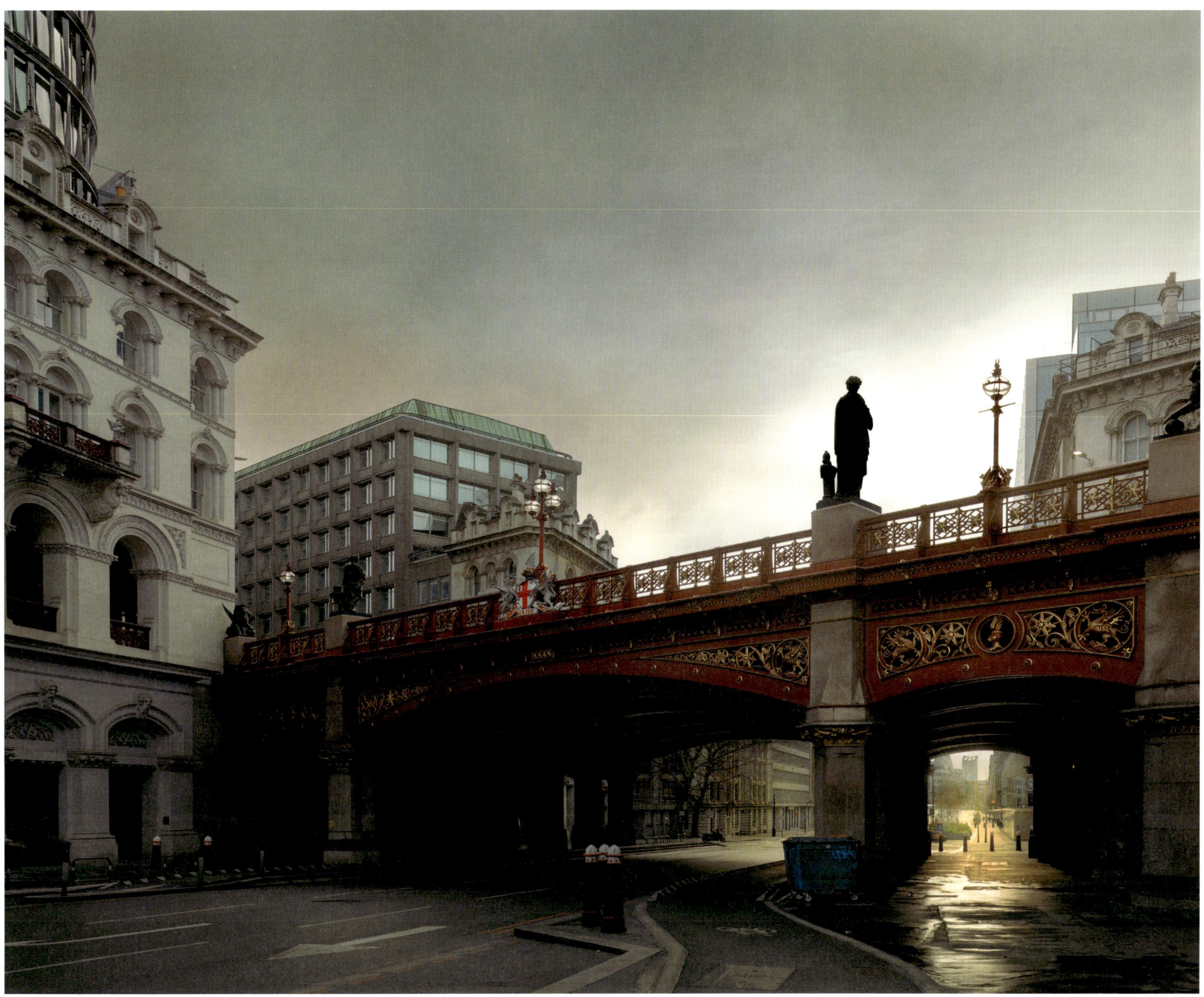

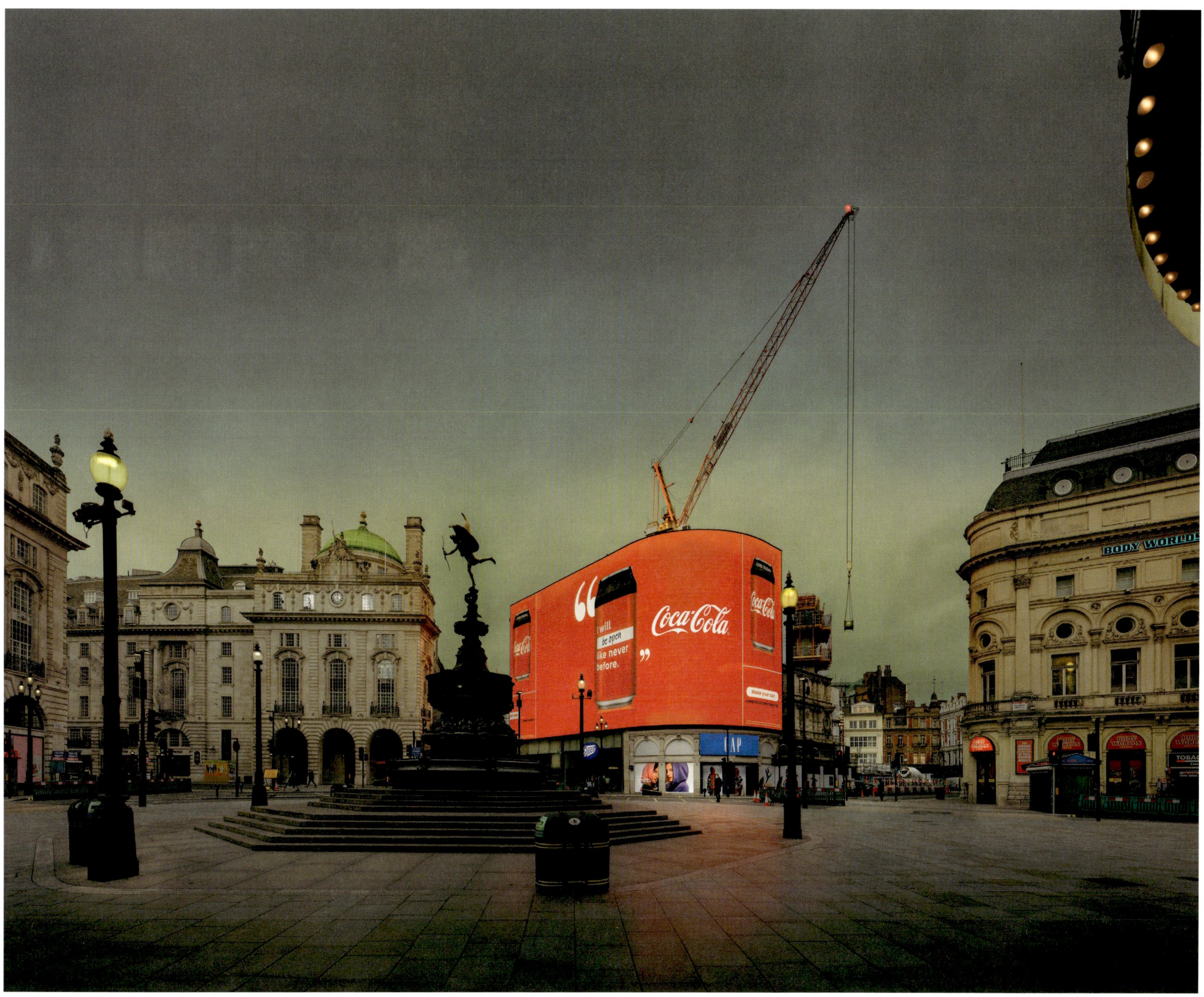
“I will be open like never before.”
Coca-Cola
ZERO SUGAR
Make your can
GAP
Boots
BODY WORLDS

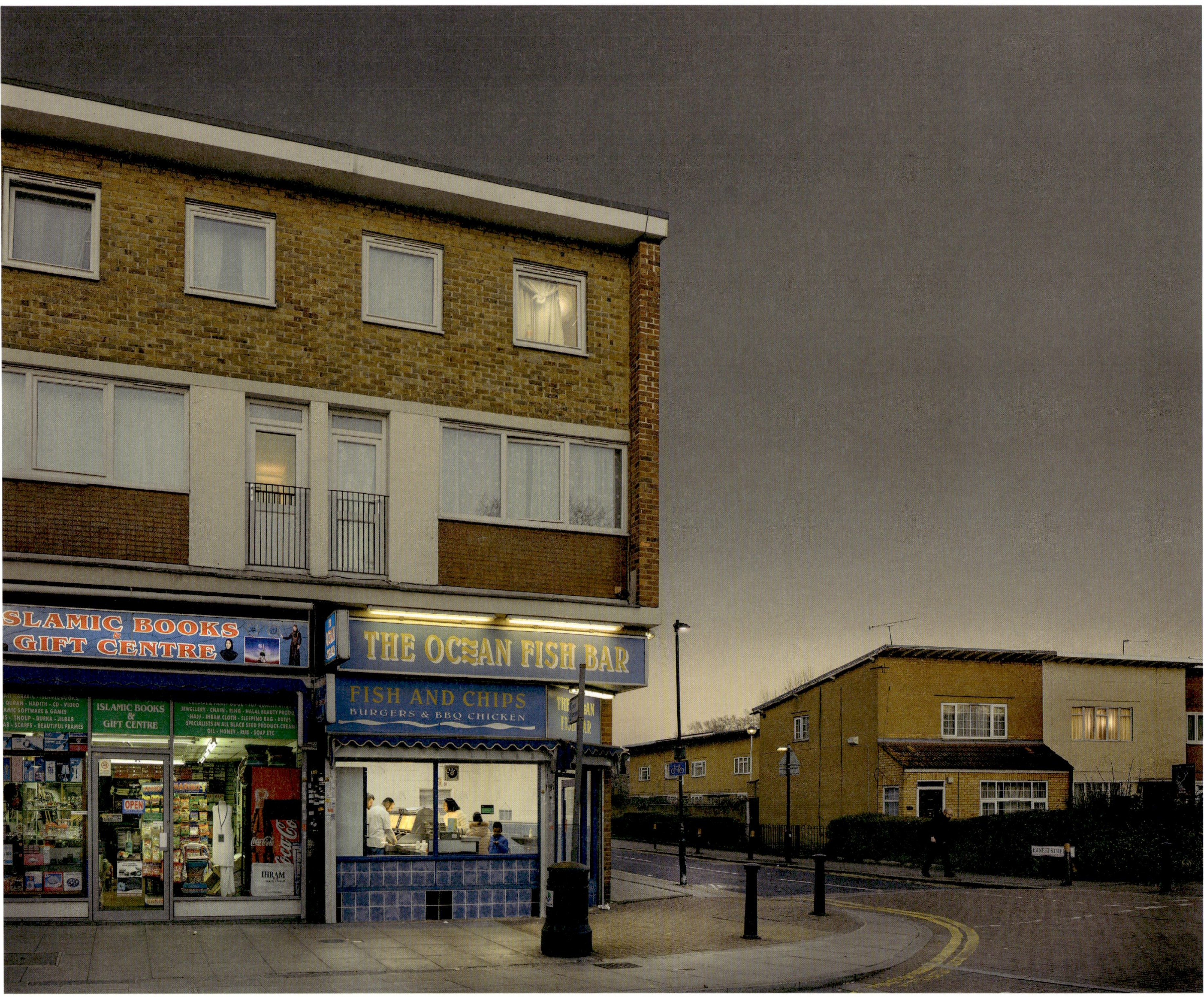

SLAMIC BOOKS
&
GIFT CENTRE
THE OCEAN FISH BAR
FISH AND CHIPS
BURGERS & BBQ CHICKEN
ISLAMIC BOOKS
&
GIFT CENTRE
OPEN
IHRAM

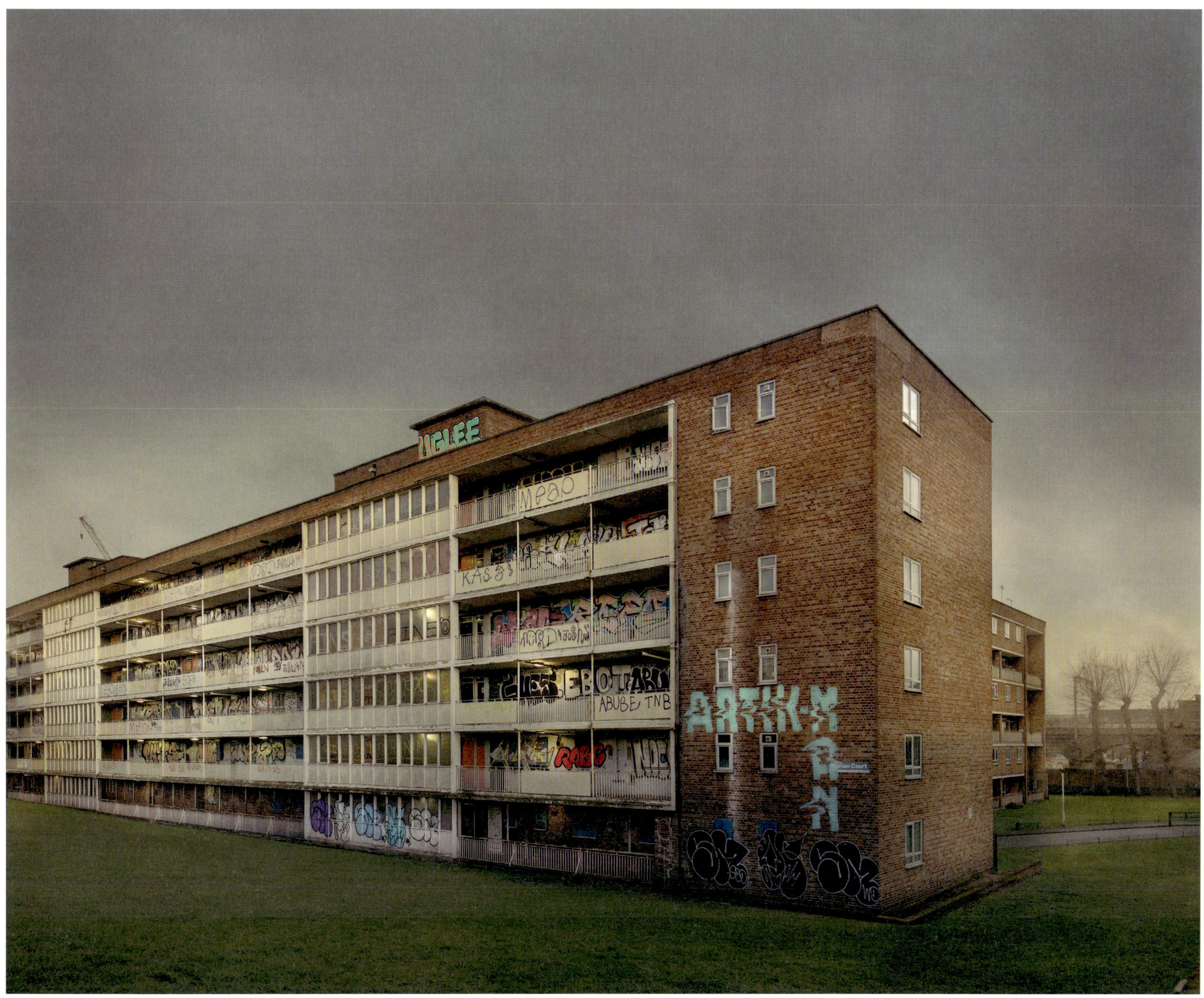

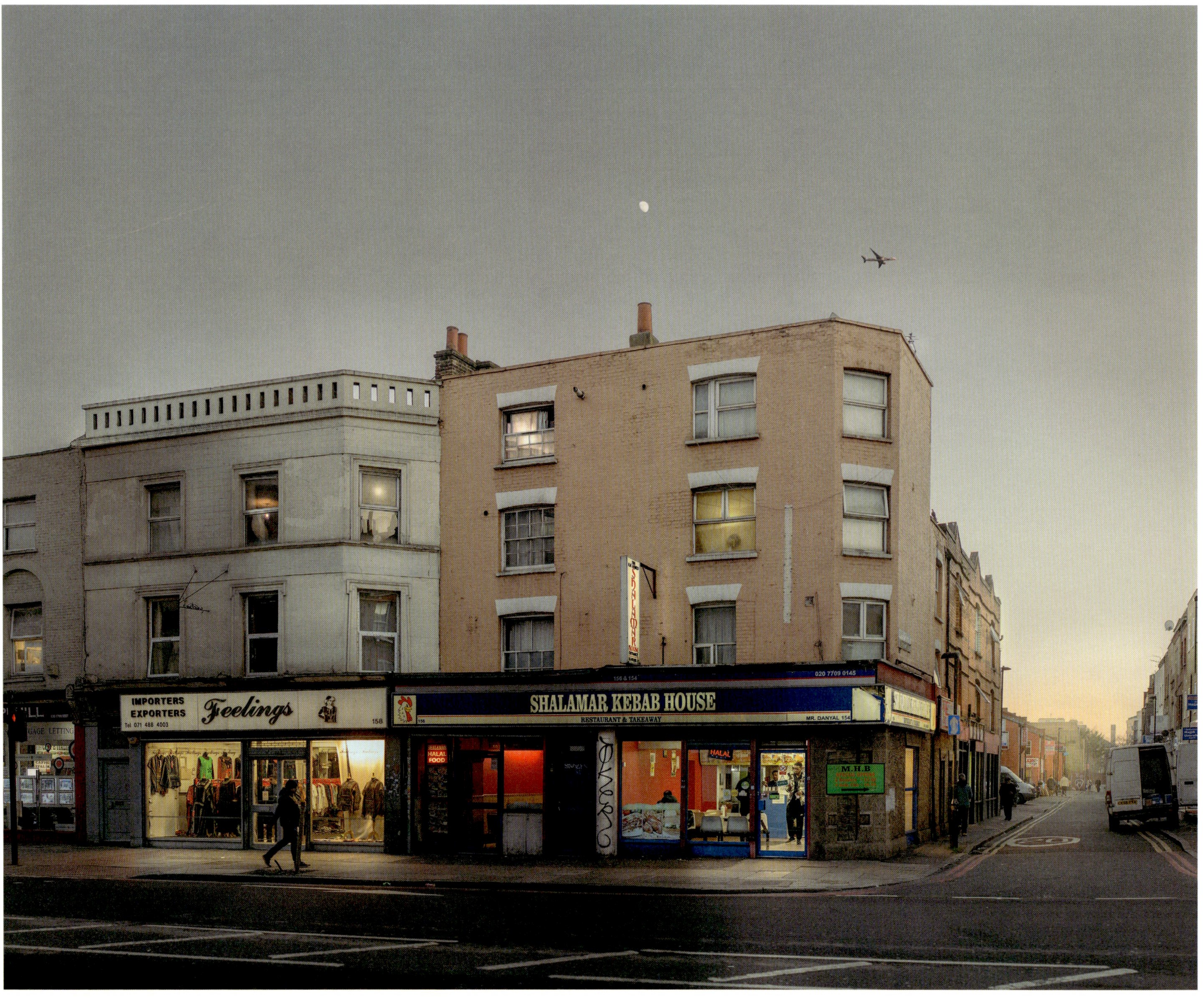
IMPORTERS
EXPORTERS
Feelings
158
SHALAMAR KEBAB HOUSE
RESTAURANT & TAKEAWAY
HALAL FOOD
HALAL
M.H.B

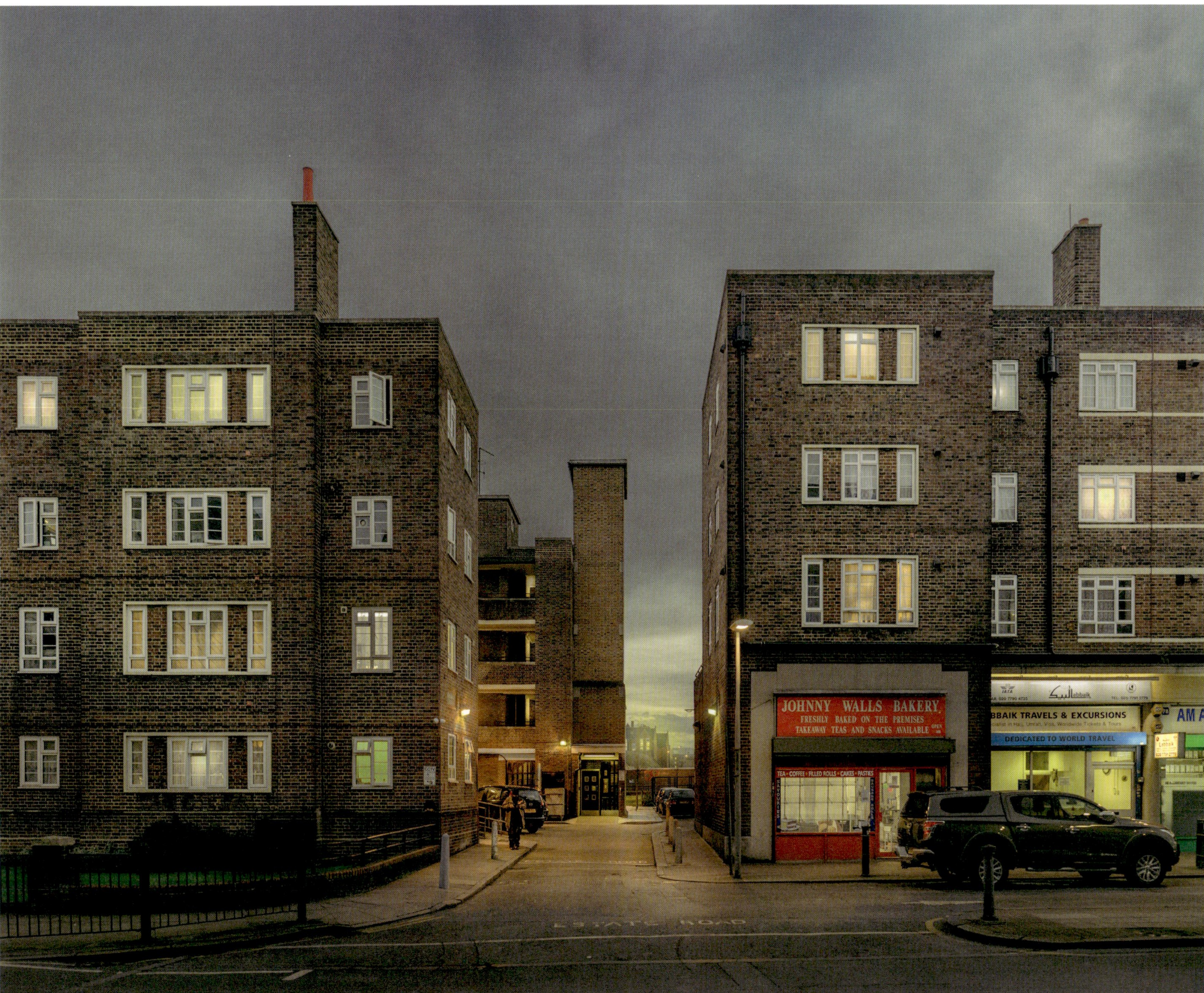
JOHNNY WALLS BAKERY
FRESHLY BAKED ON THE PREMISES
TAKEAWAY TEAS AND SNACKS AVAILABLE
TEA • COFFEE • FILLED ROLLS • CAKES • PASTIES
SAVOURIES
IATA
TEL: 020 7791 2779
BBAIK TRAVELS & EXCURSIONS
DEDICATED TO WORLD TRAVEL
AM A
ESTATE ROAD

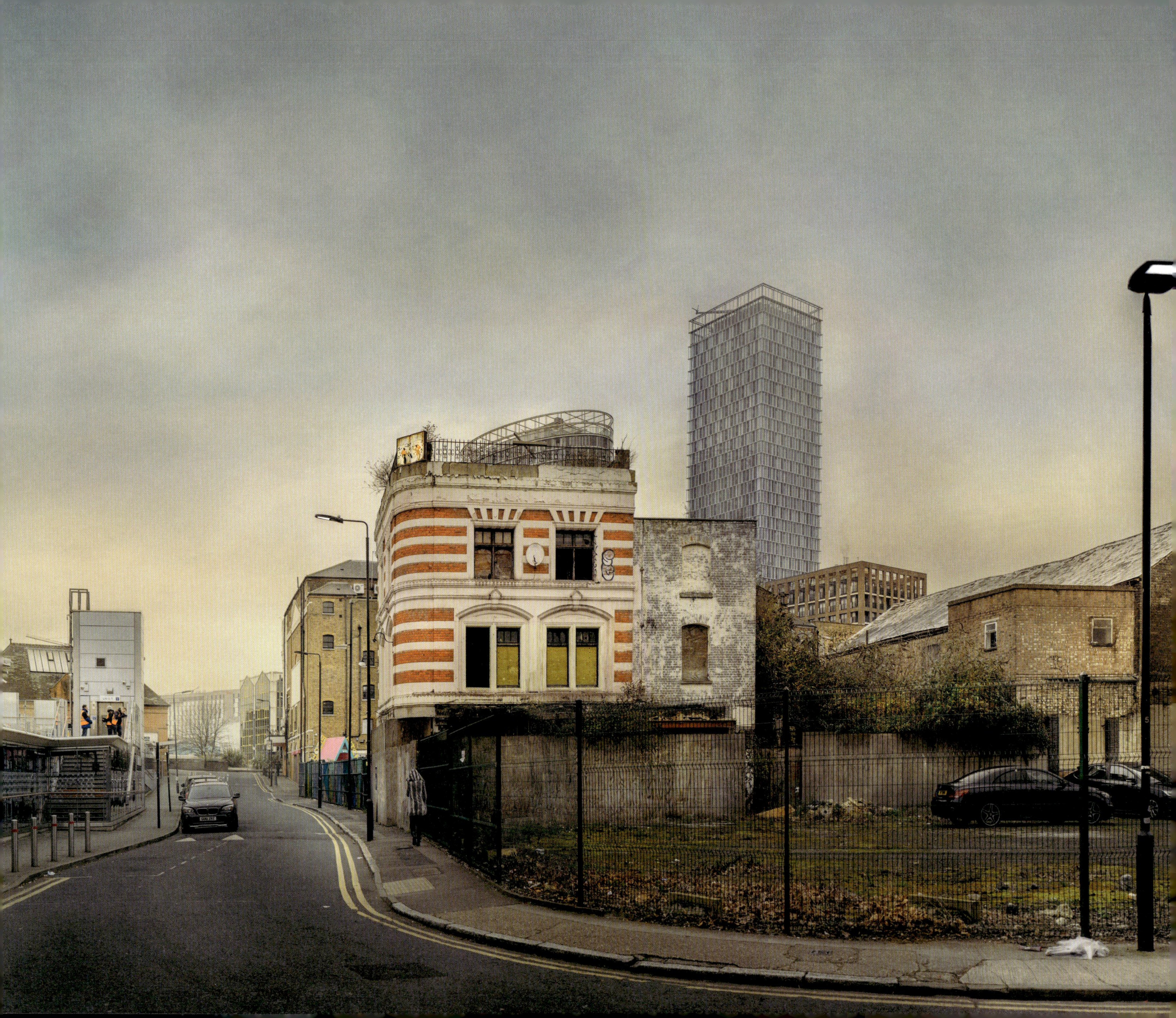

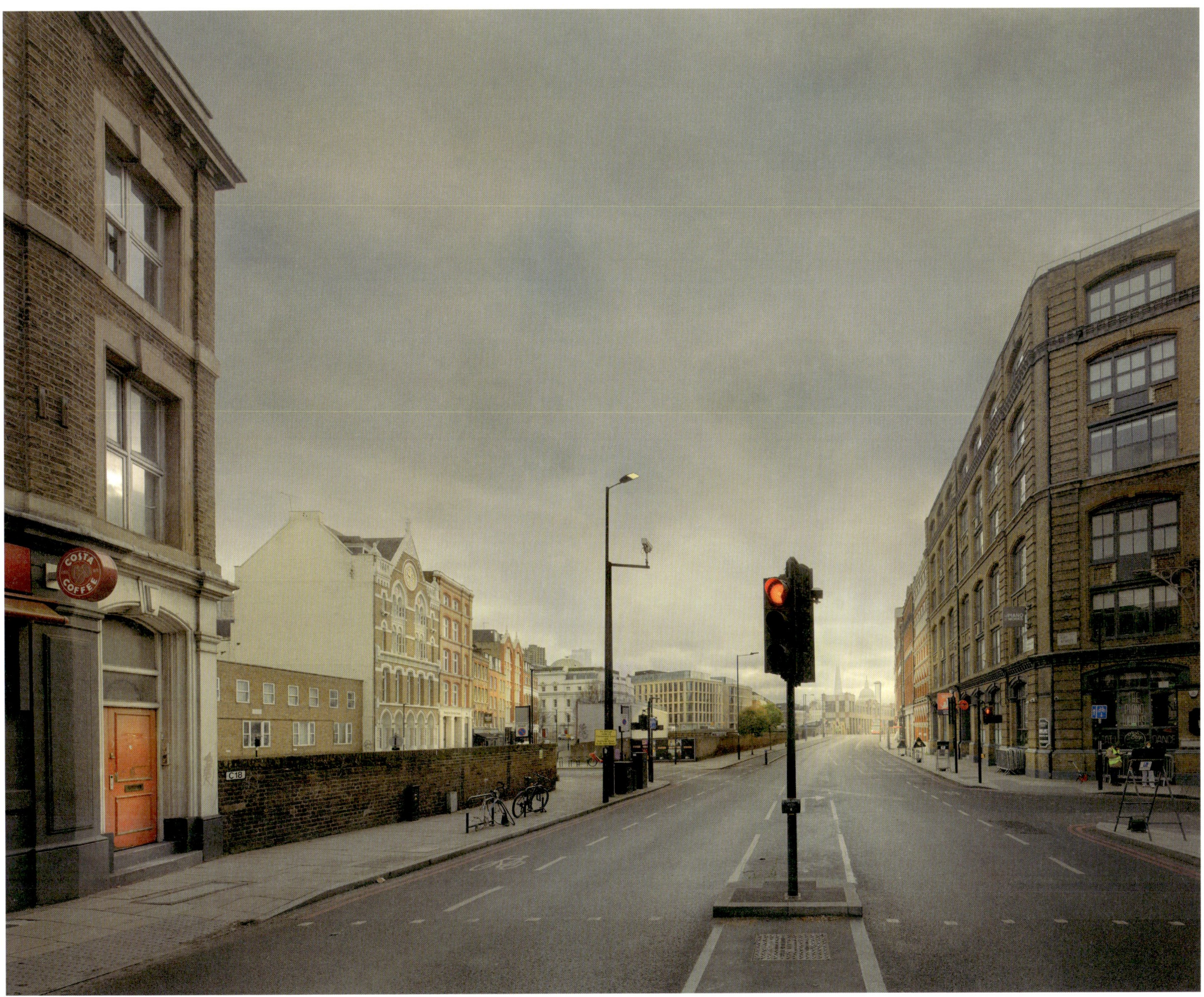
COSTA
COFFEE
C18

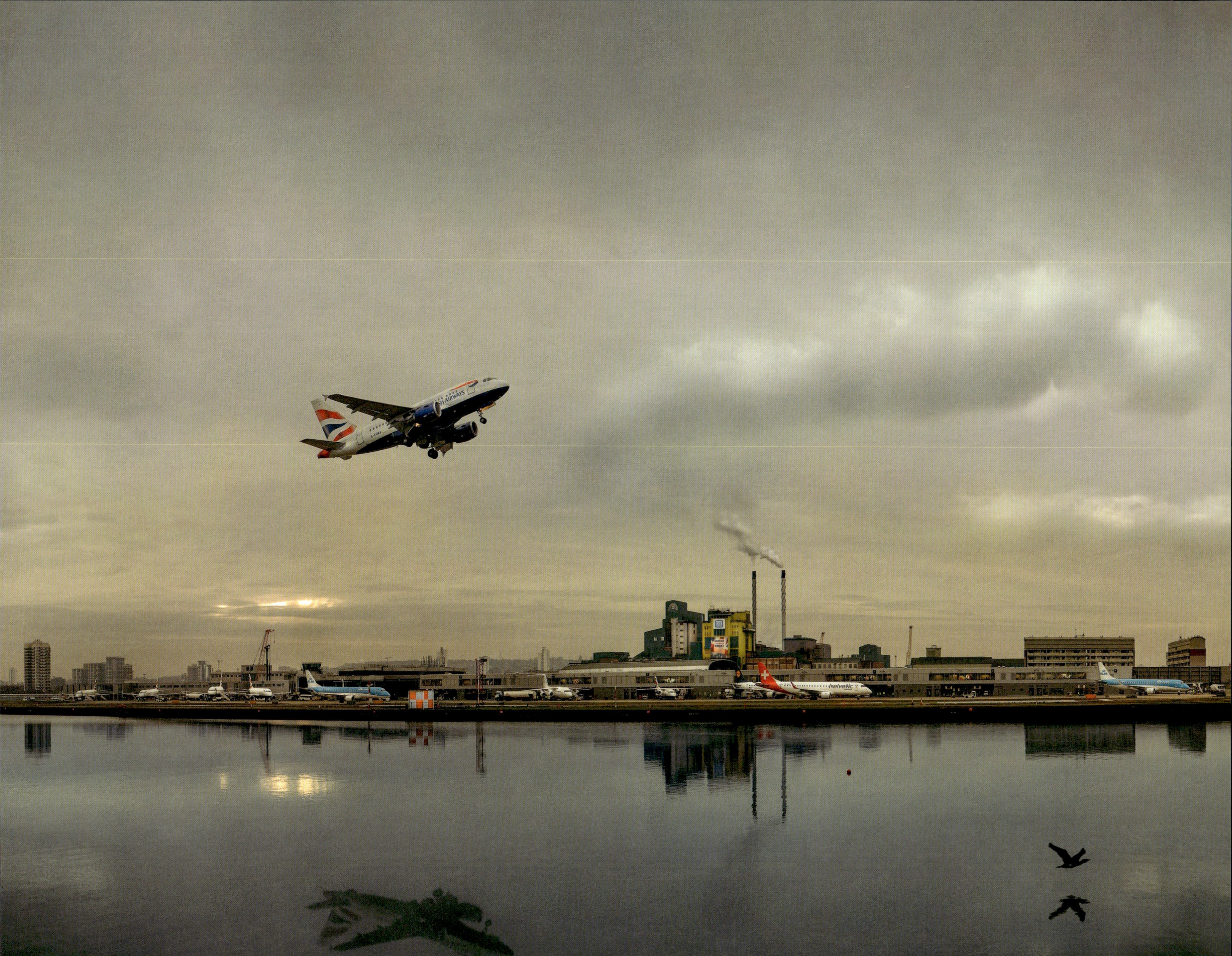
helvetic

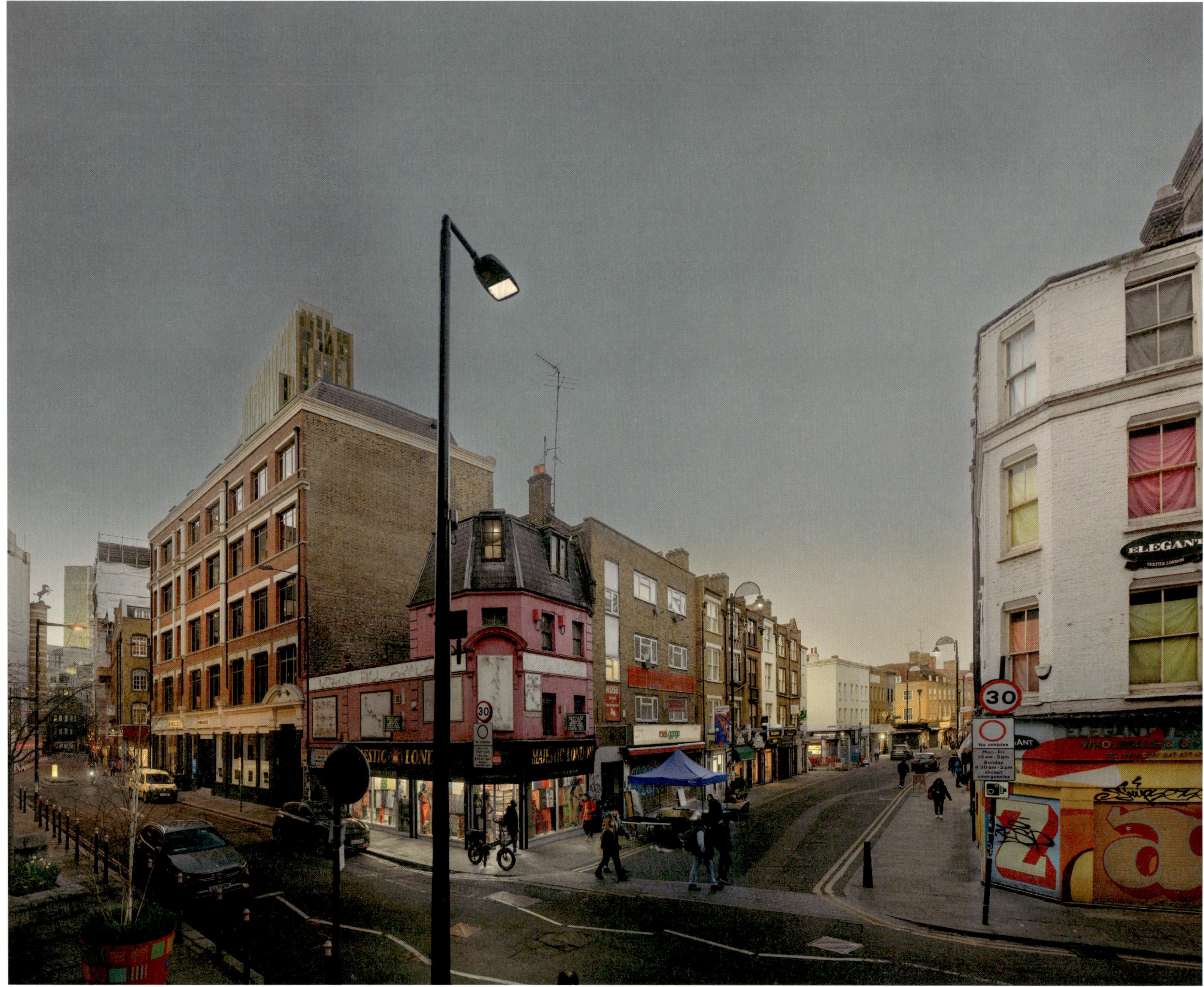

ELEGANT
TEXTILE LONDON
30
No vehicles
Mon - Fri
10 am - 2 pm
Sunday
6:30 am - 2 pm
except
emergencies

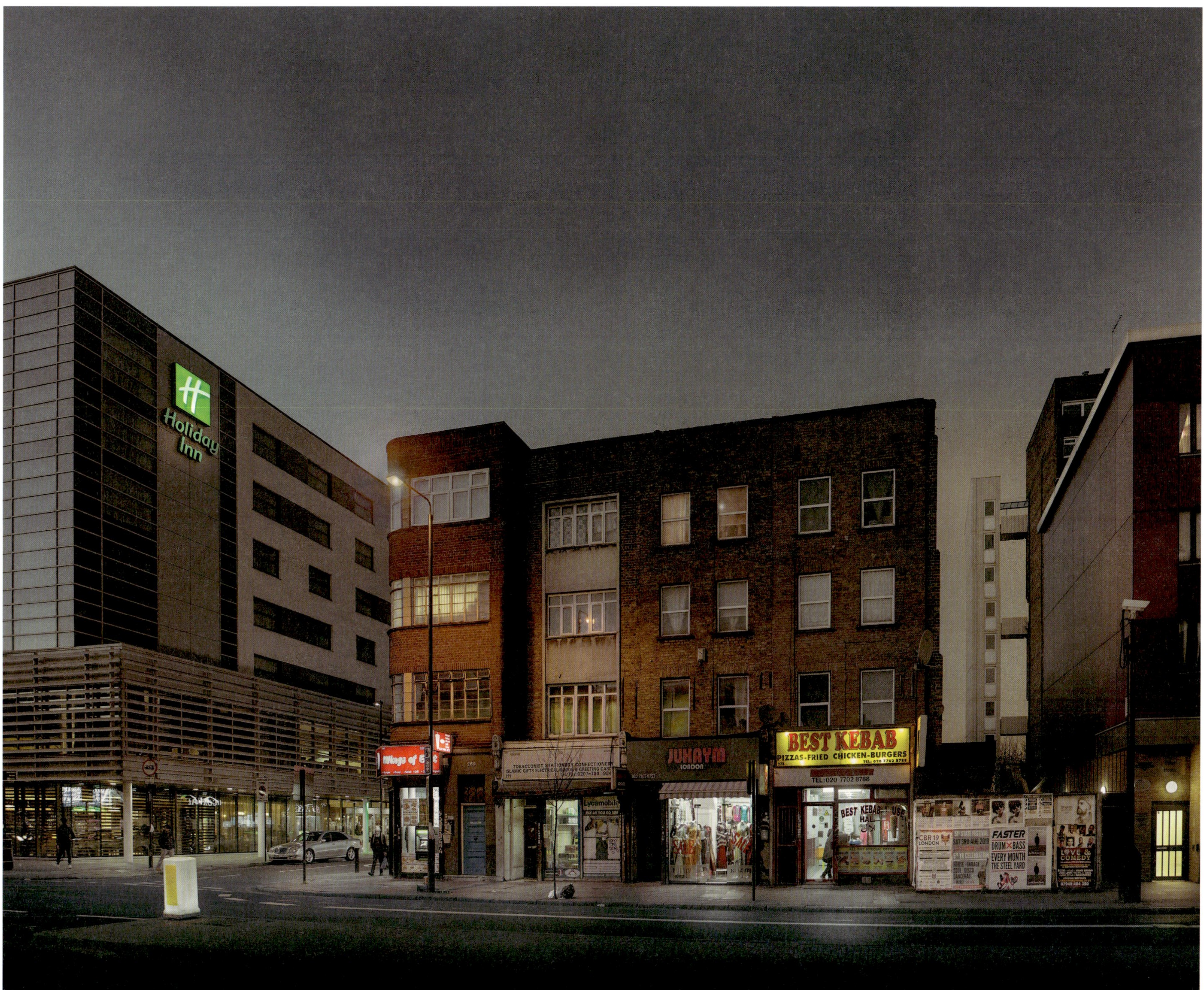
Holiday Inn
TOBACCONIST STATIONERY CONFECTIONERY
ISLAMIC GIFTS ELECTRICAL GOODS & GREETING CARDS
Lycamobile
PAY AS YOU GO SIM
JUHAYM
LONDON
020 7265 8753
BEST KEBAB
PIZZAS-FRIED CHICKEN-BURGERS
TEL: 020 7702 8788
TEL:020 7702 8788
CBR 19
LONDON
SAT 3RD AUG 2019
HOUSE · GARAGE
SOUL · DISCO
DANCEHALL
FASTER
DRUM×BASS
EVERY MONTH
THE STEEL YARD
LOVE & COMEDY
07949 484 350

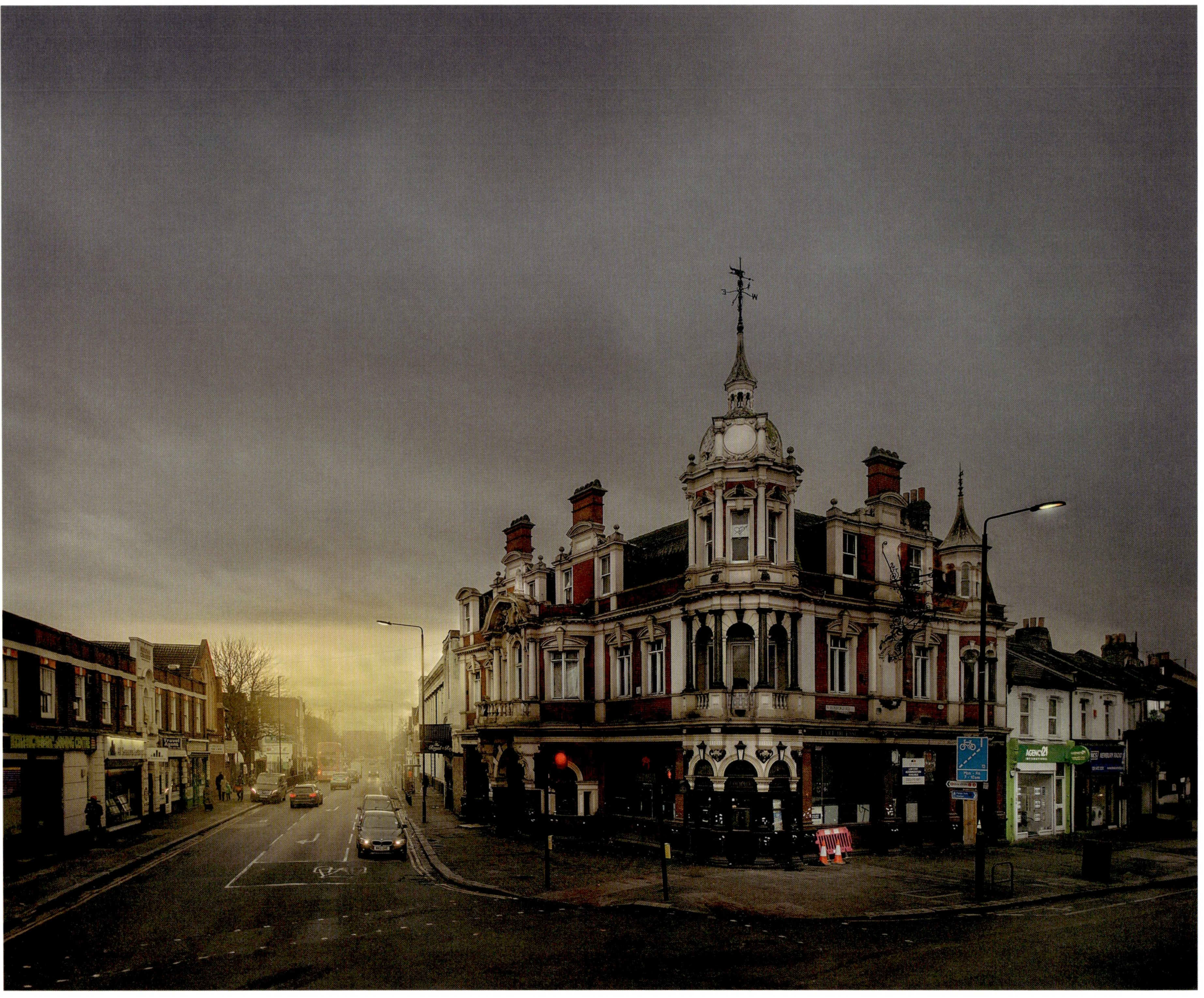

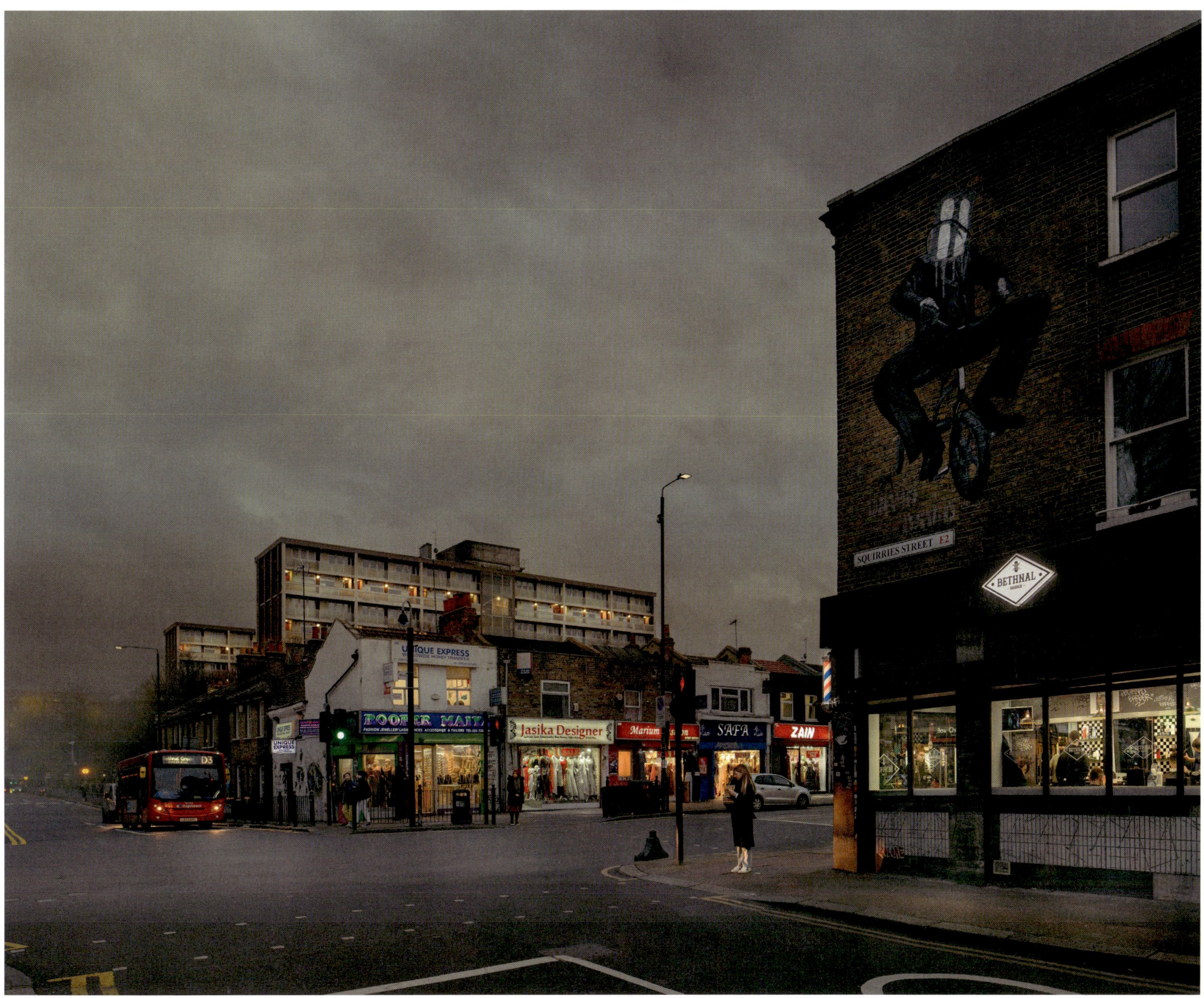

SQUIRRIES STREET E2
BETHNAL
UNIQUE EXPRESS
Jasika Designer
SAFA
ZAIN
D3

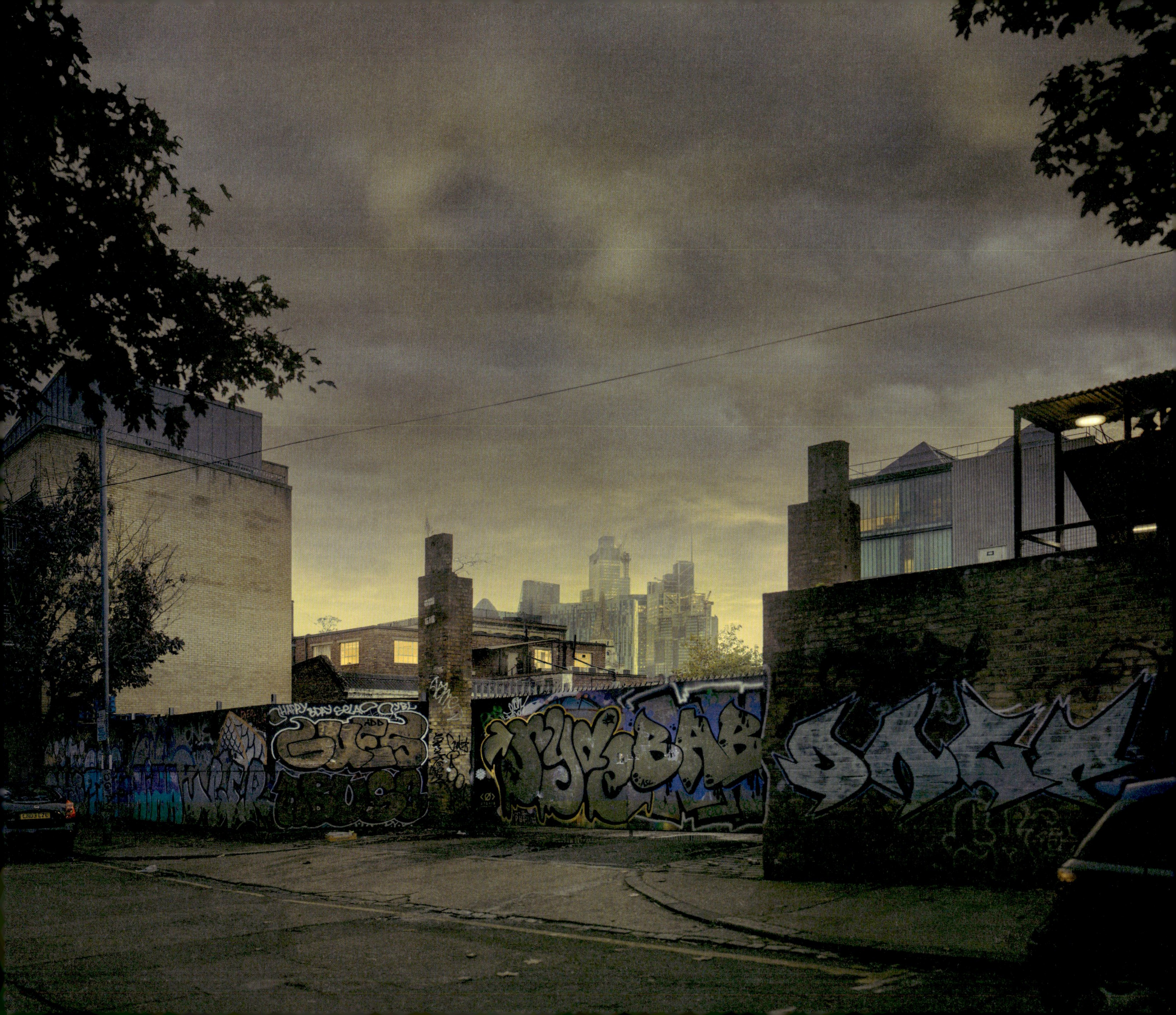

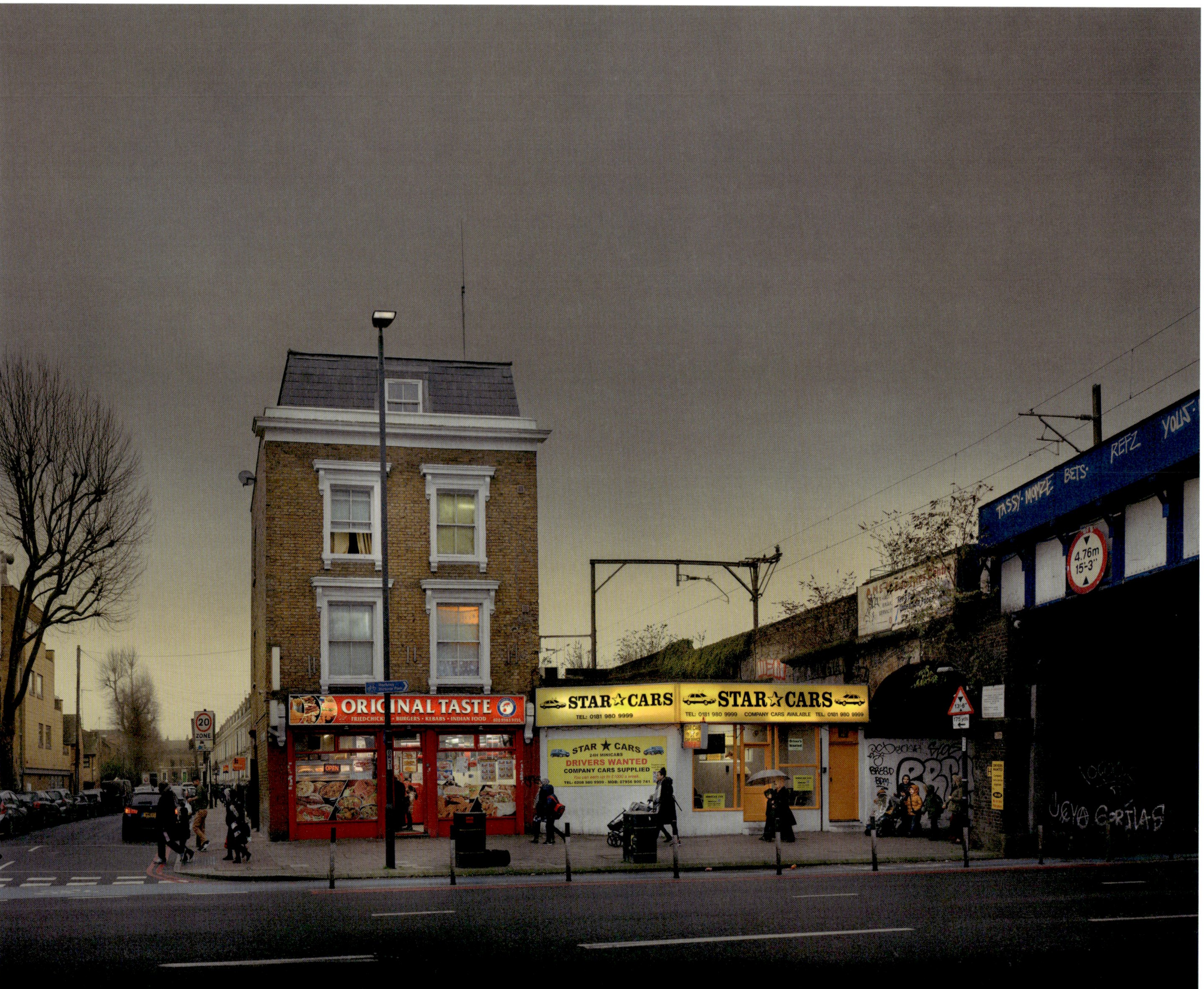
ORIGINAL TASTE
BURGERS • KEBABS • INDIAN FOOD
OPEN
STAR CARS
TEL: 0181 980 9999
STAR CARS
TEL: 0181 980 9999 COMPANY CARS AVAILABLE TEL: 0181 980 9999
STAR CARS
24H MINICABS
DRIVERS WANTED
COMPANY CARS SUPPLIED
You can earn up to £1000 a week
TEL: 0208 980 9999 - MOB: 07956 900 741
Driver's Wanted
20
ZONE
4.76m
15'-3"
TASSY MONZE BETS REFZ YOUS

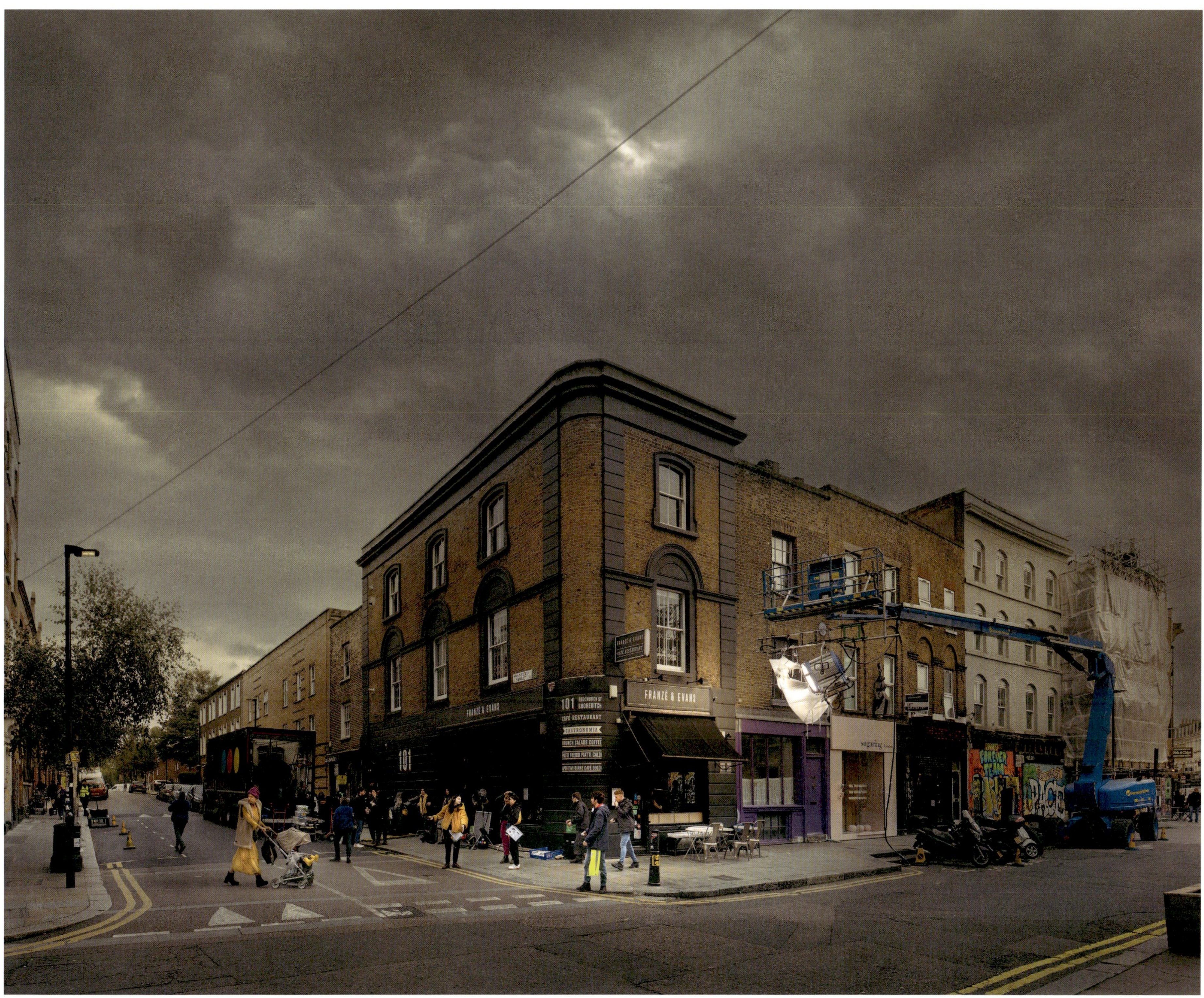
FRANZÈ & EVANS
CAFÉ RESTAURANT
FRANZÈ & EVANS
101 REDCHURCH ST SHOREDITCH
CAFÉ RESTAURANT
GASTRONOMIA
BRUNCH SALADS COFFEE
PIATTI FREDDI PIATTI CALDI
APERITIVI BIRRE CAFÉ DOLCI
FRANZÈ & EVANS
101
sugaring

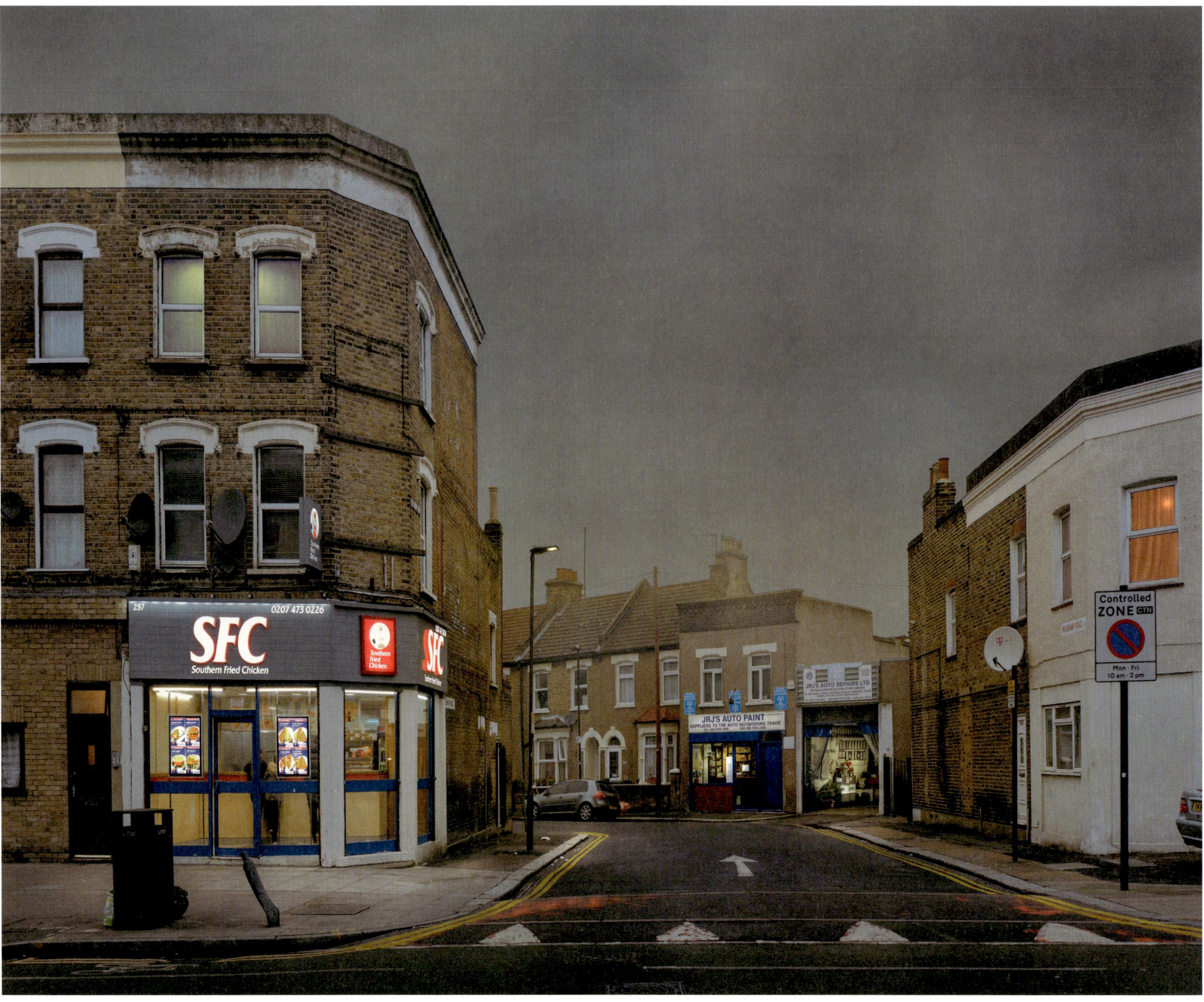
257
0207 473 0226
SFC
Southern Fried Chicken
Southern Fried Chicken
SFC
JRJ'S AUTO PAINT
SUPPLIERS TO THE AUTO REFINISHING TRADE
JRJ'S AUTO REPAIRS LTD
Controlled
ZONE CTN
Mon - Fri
10 am - 2 pm

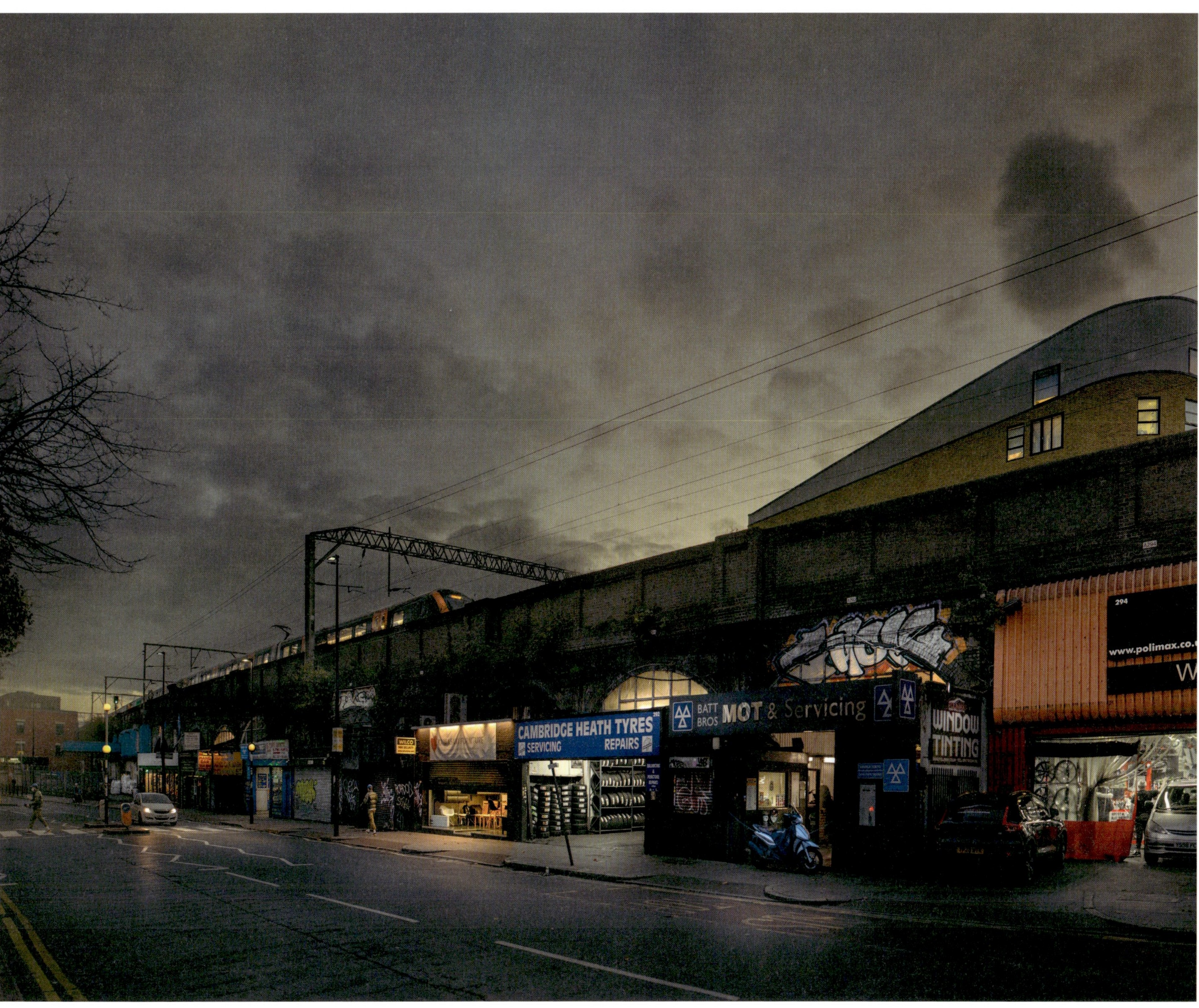
CAMBRIDGE HEATH TYRES
SERVICING
REPAIRS
BATT BROS
MOT & Servicing
WINDOW TINTING
294

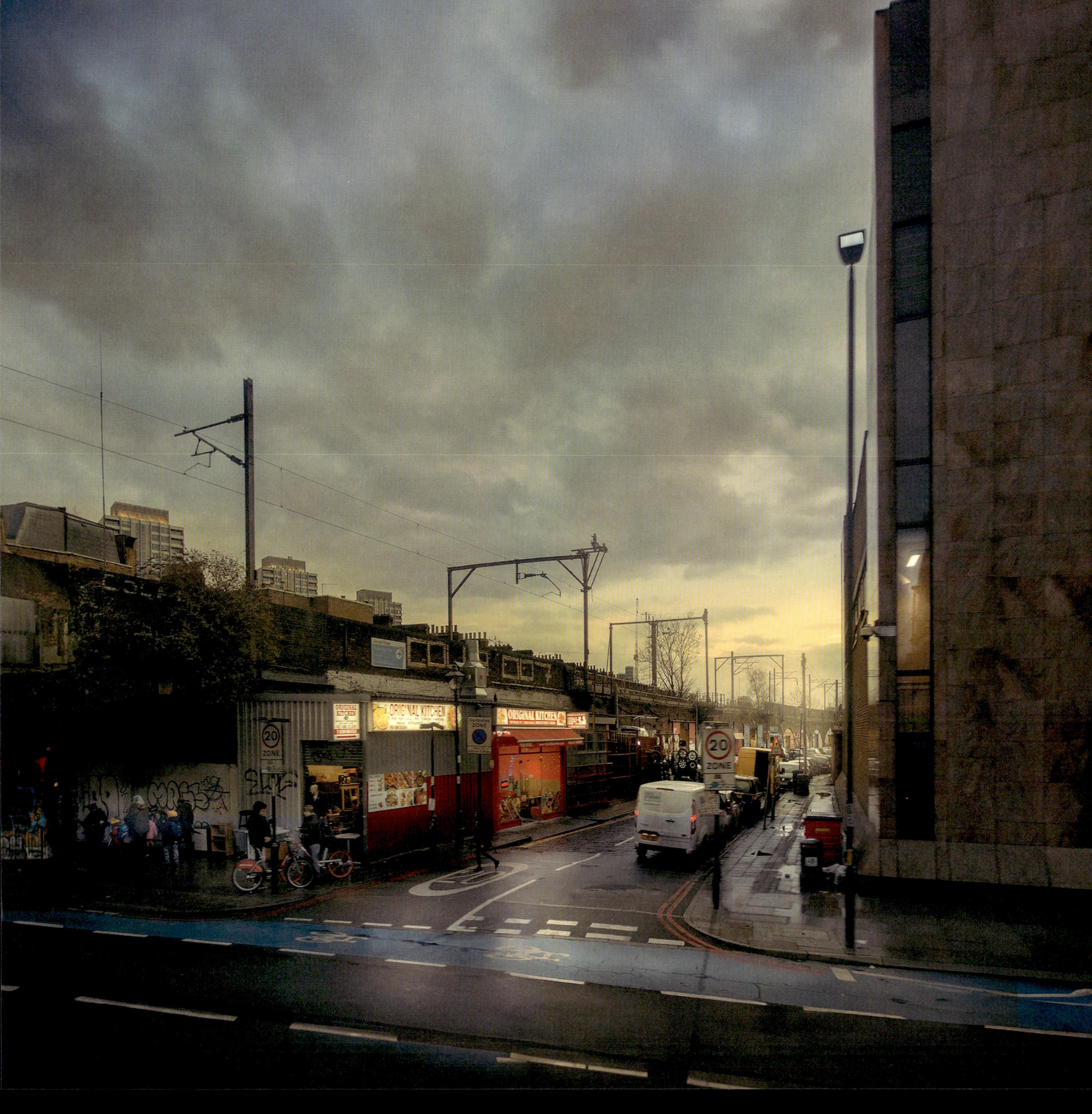
ORIGINAL KITCHEN
ORIGINAL KITCHEN
20
ZONE
20
ZONE

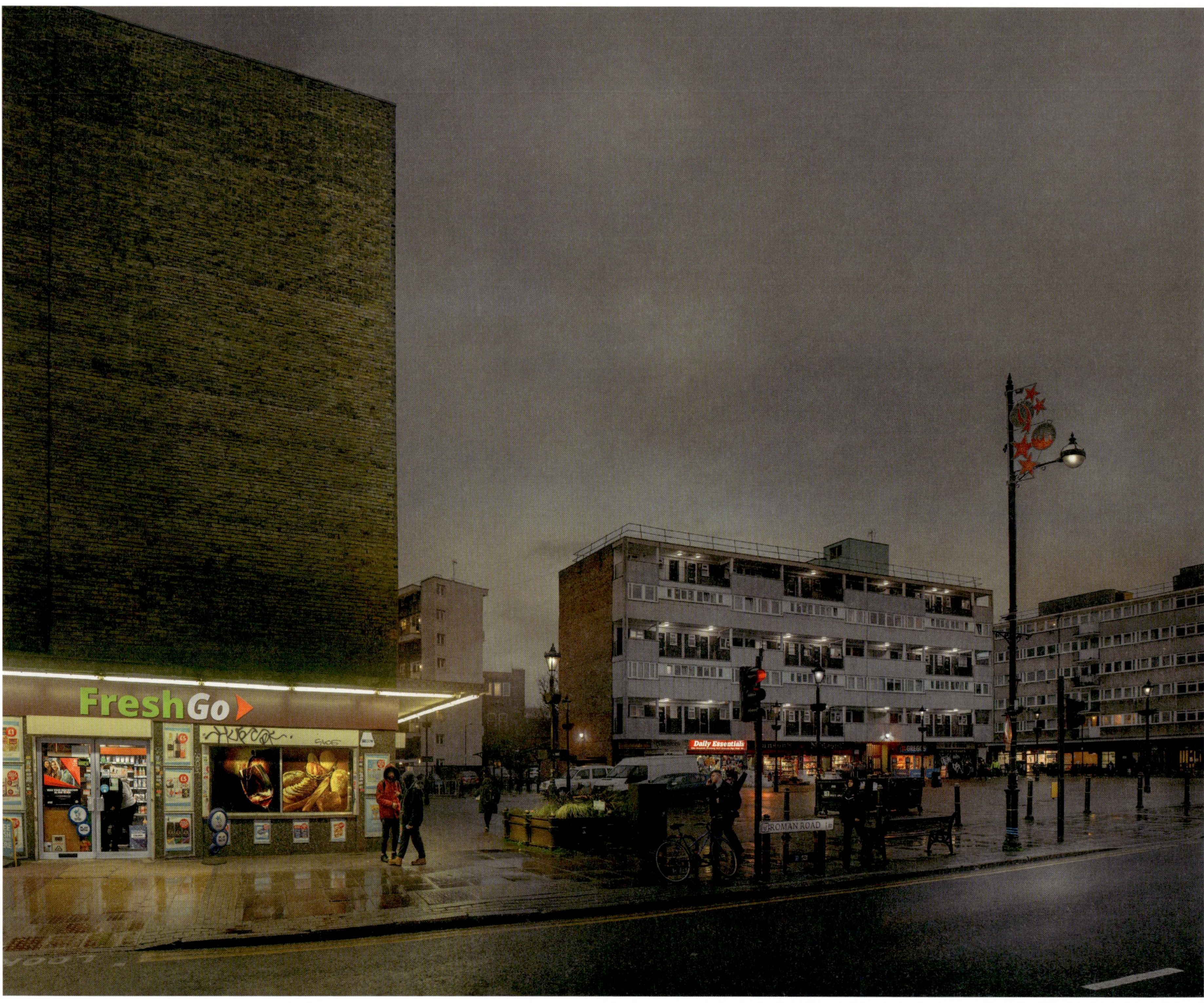
FreshGo
Daily Essentials
ROMAN ROAD

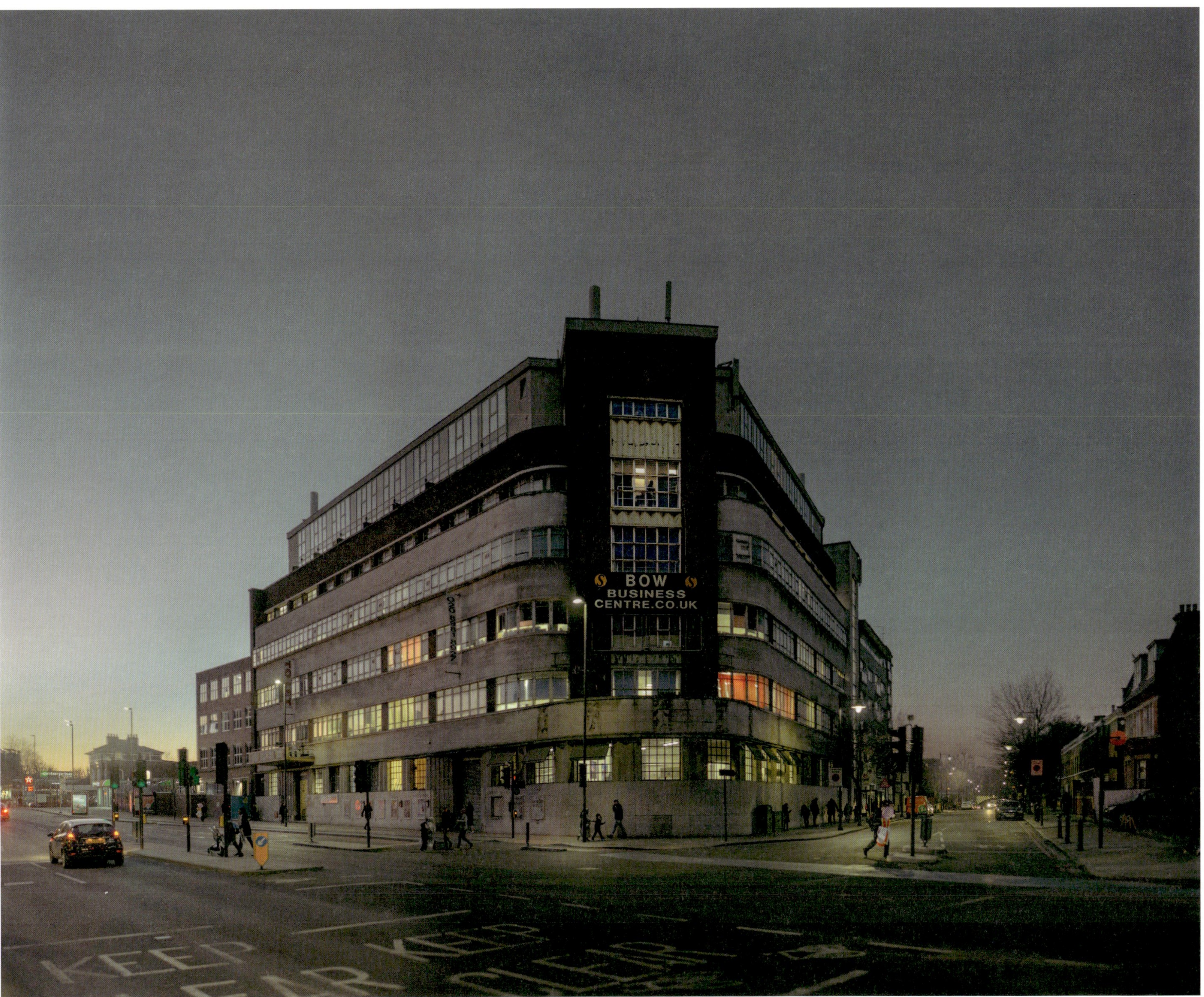
BOW
BUSINESS
CENTRE.CO.UK
KEEP CLEAR
KEEP CLEAR

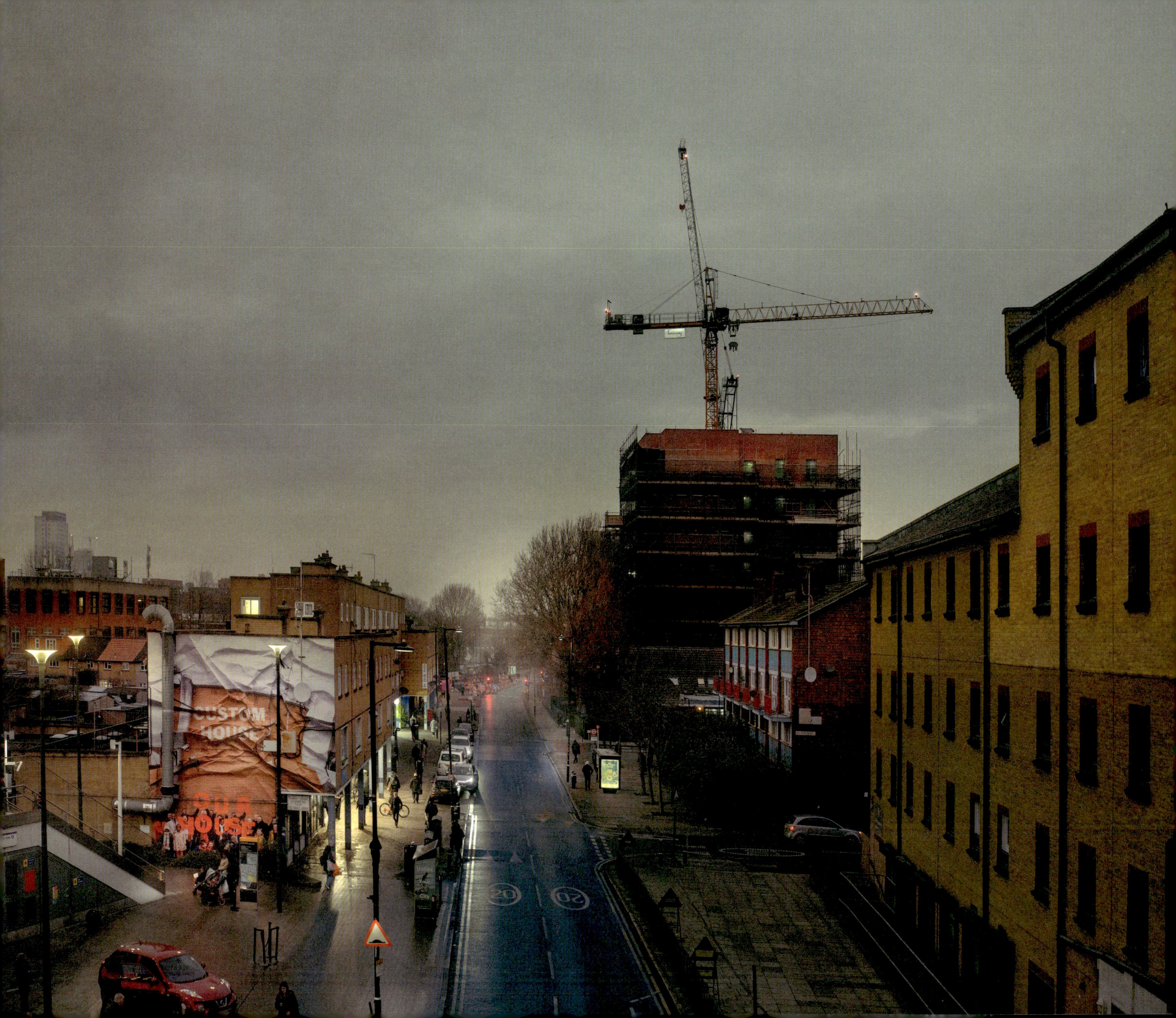
CUSTOM
HOUSE
OUR
HOUSE
20
20

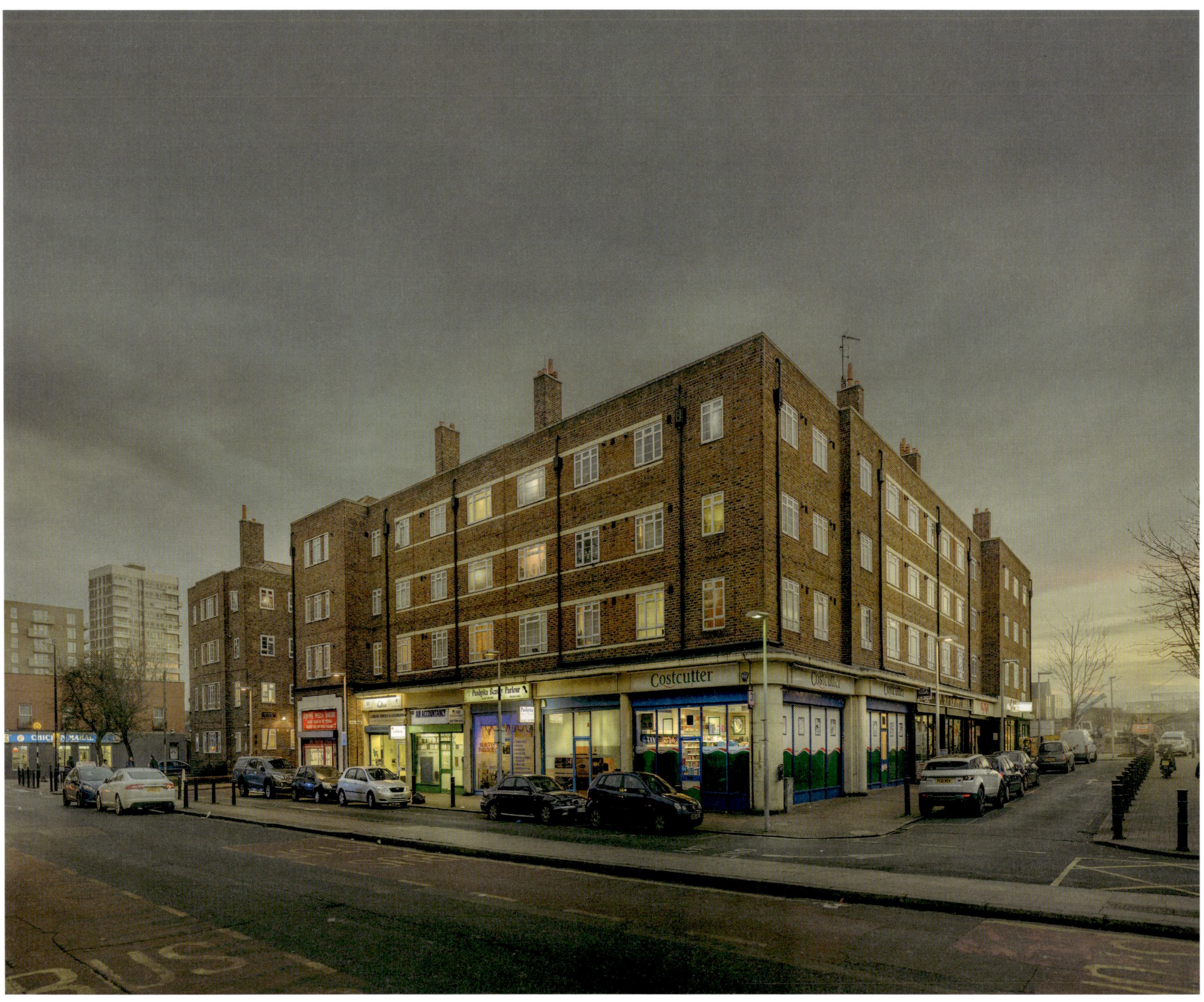
Costcutter
Pushpita

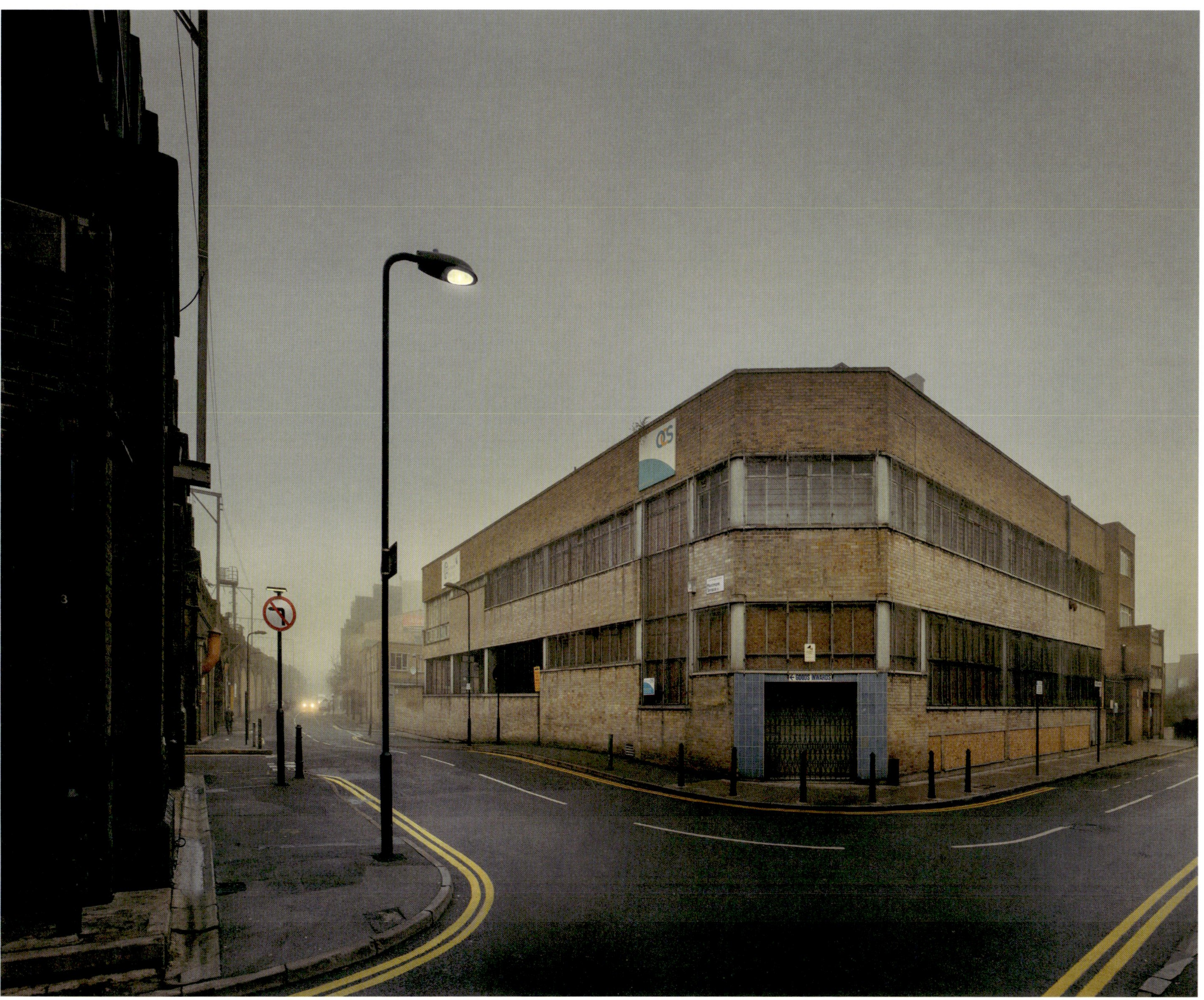
OCS
← GOODS INWARDS

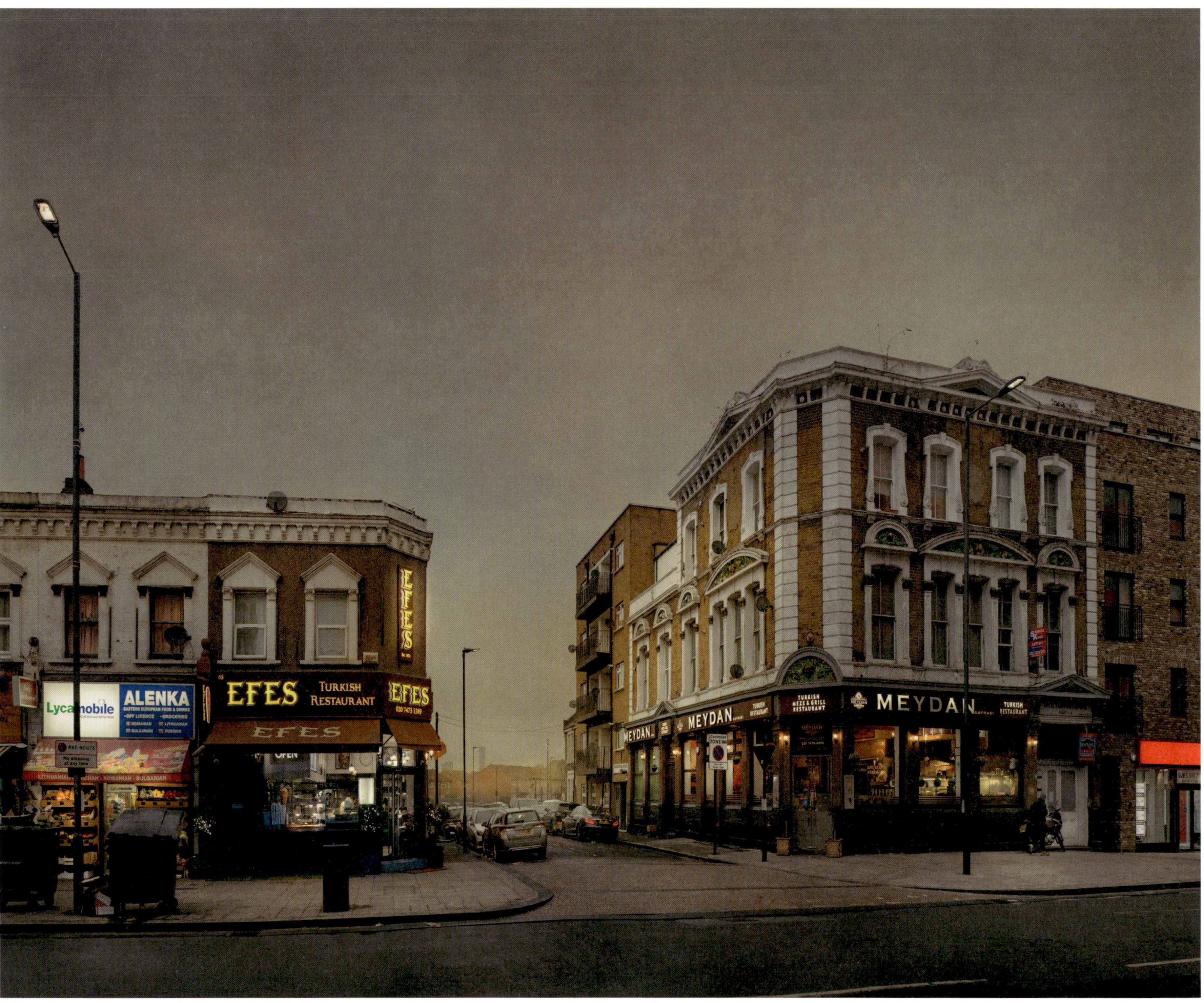
EFES
EFES
TURKISH
RESTAURANT
EFES
EFES
ALENKA
Lycamobile
MEYDAN
MEYDAN
MEYDAN
TURKISH
RESTAURANT
TURKISH
MEZE & GRILL
RESTAURANT

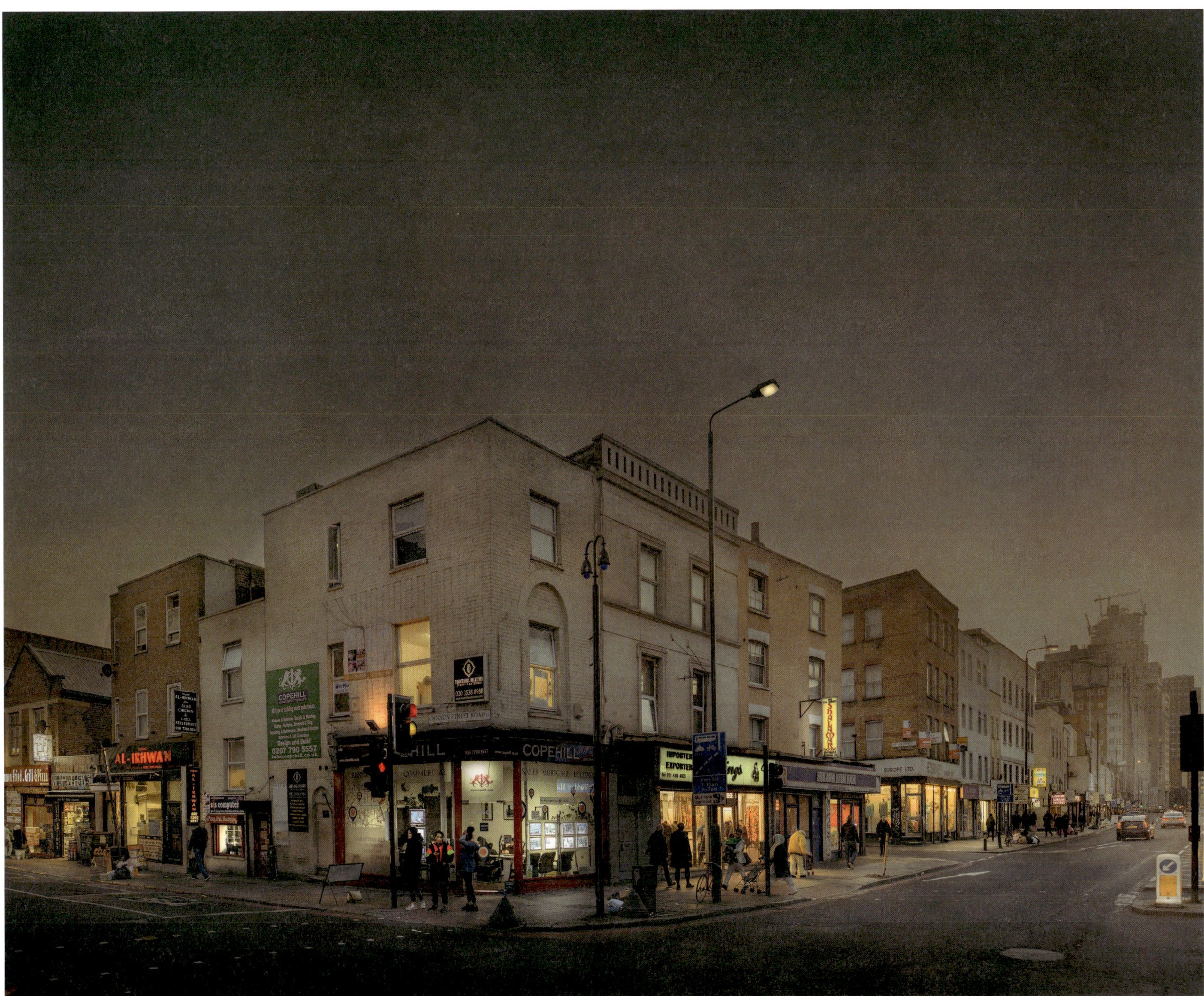
COPEHILL
Design and Build
0207 790 5557
info@copehill.co.uk
TRADITIONAL OCCASIONS
EVENTS & CATERING
020 3538 8988
CANNON STREET ROAD
COPEHILL
COMMERCIAL
SALES MORTGAGE LETTINGS
AL-IKHWAN

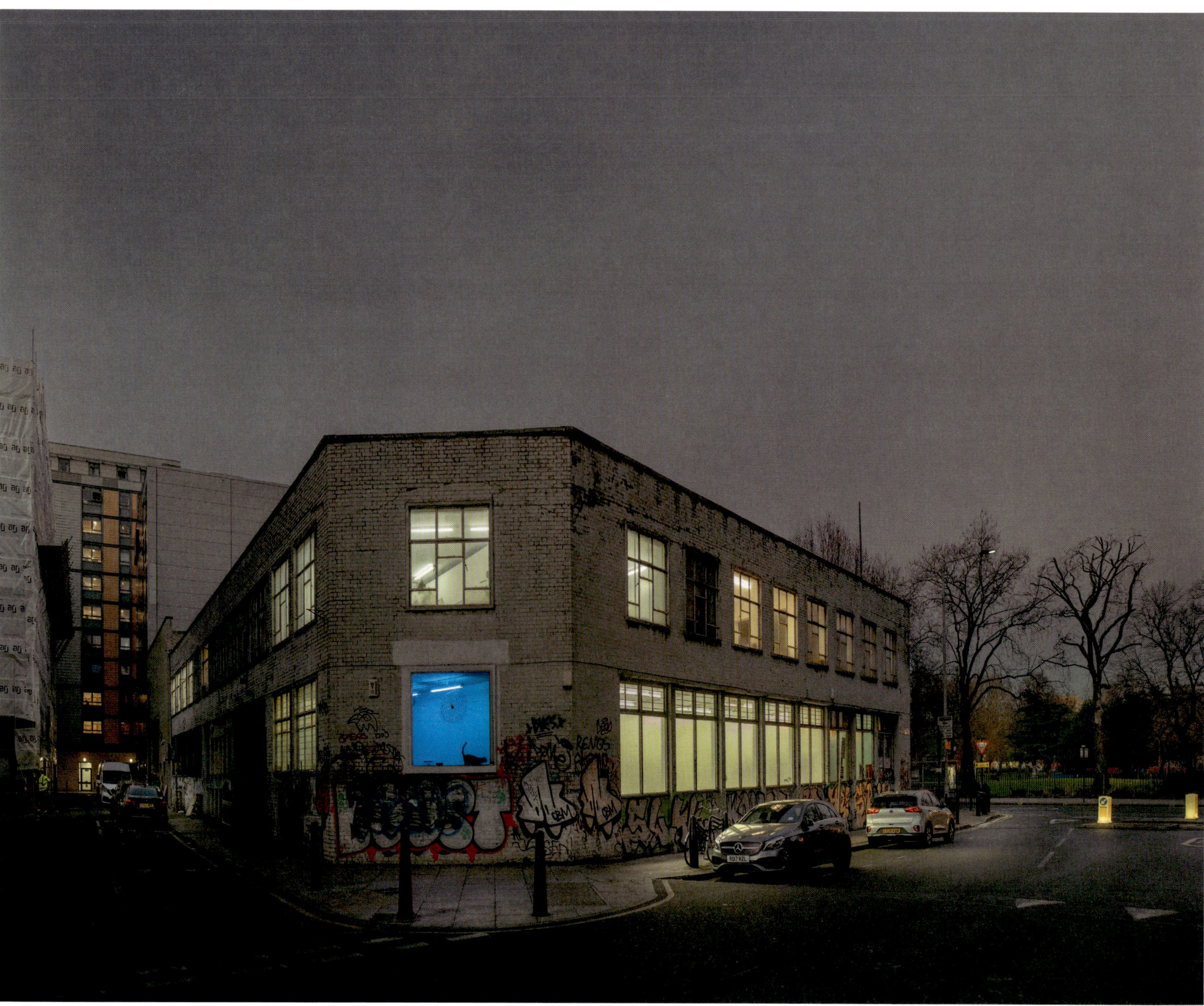

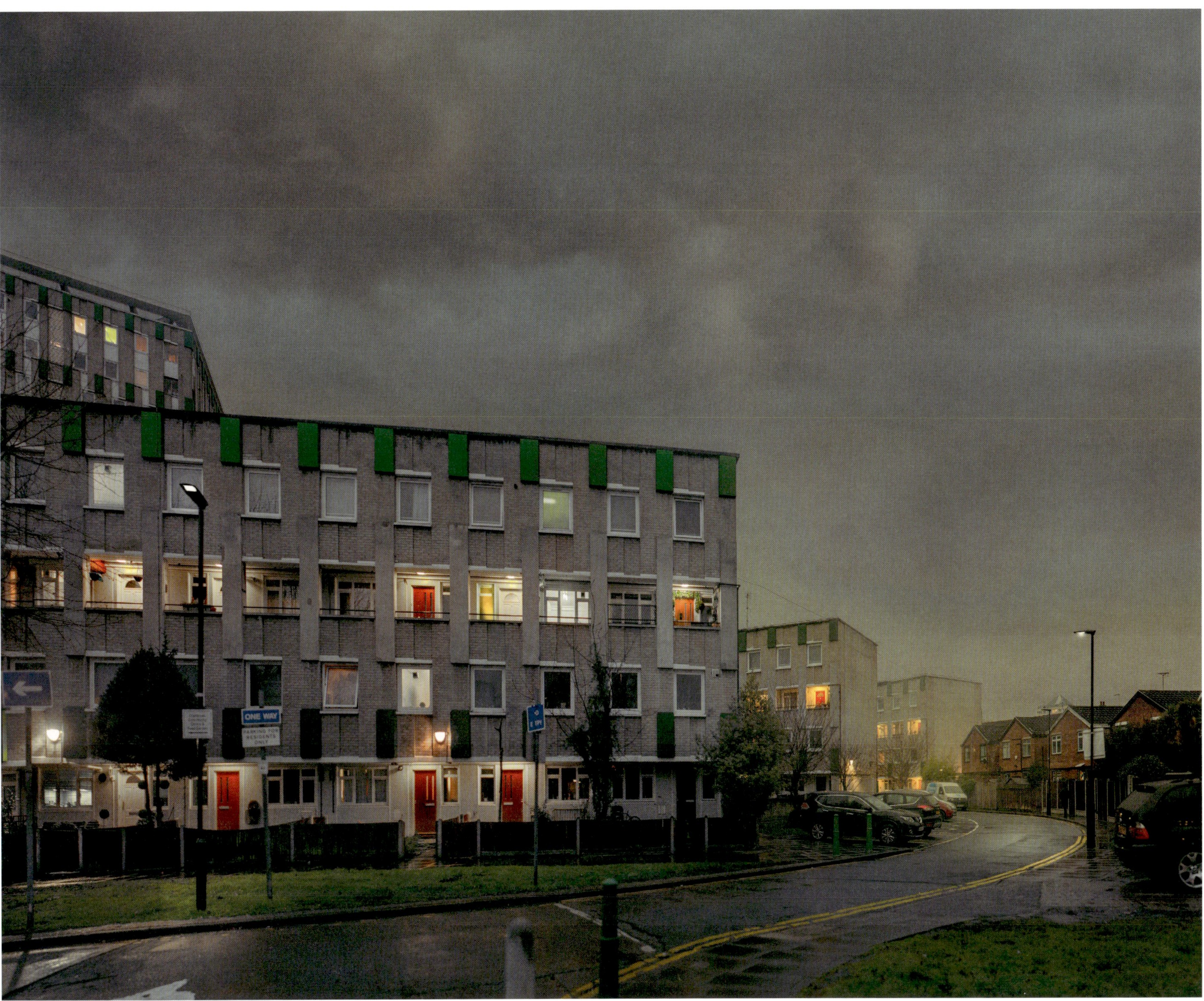
ONE WAY
PARKING FOR
RESIDENTS
ONLY

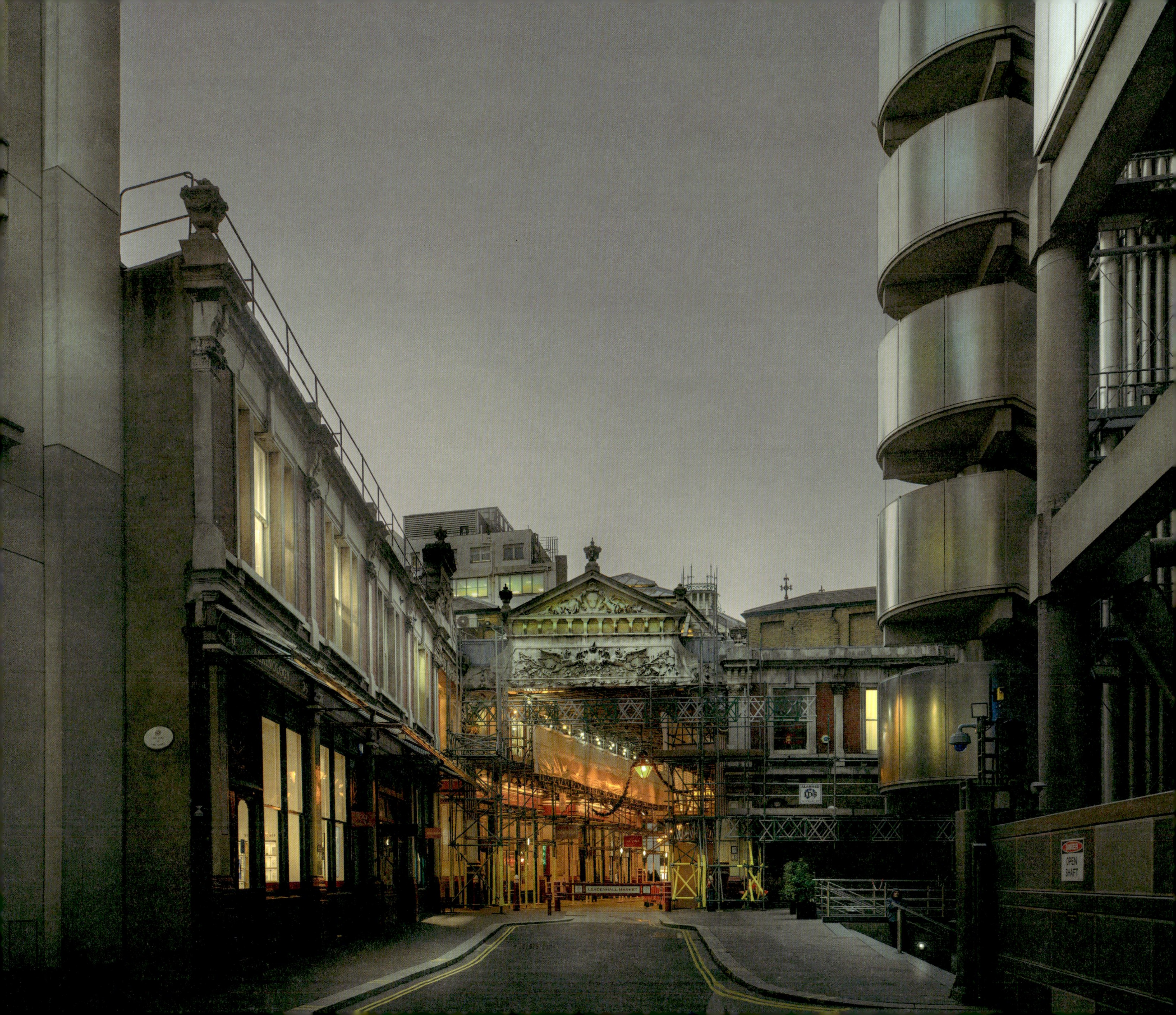
LEADENHALL MARKET
OPEN SHAFT

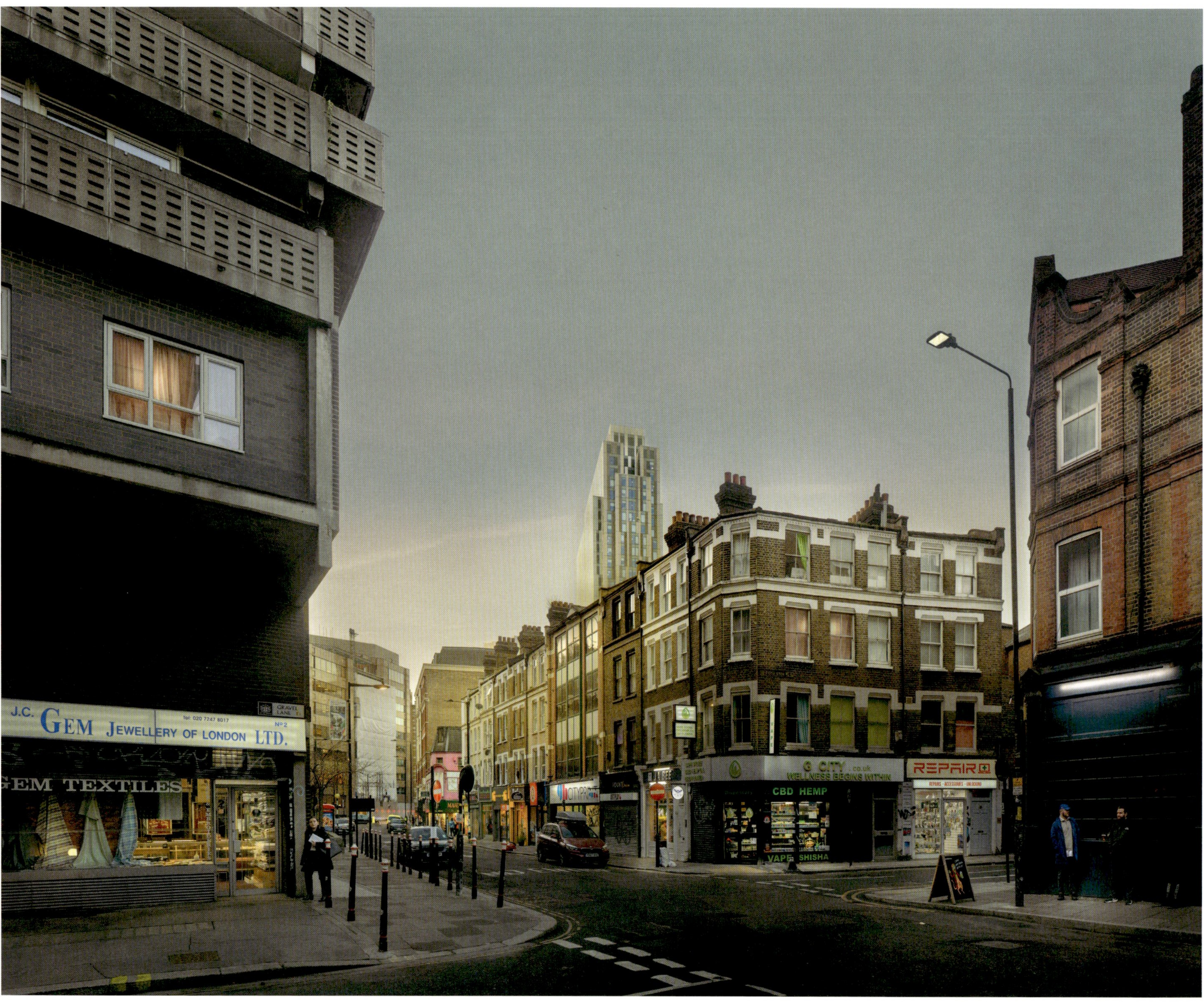
J.C. GEM JEWELLERY OF LONDON LTD.
Tel: 020 7247 8017
Nº2
GRAVEL LANE
GEM TEXTILES
G CITY .co.uk
WELLNESS BEGINS WITHIN
CBD HEMP
VAPE SHISHA
REPAIR
REPAIRS · ACCESSORIES · UNLOCKING

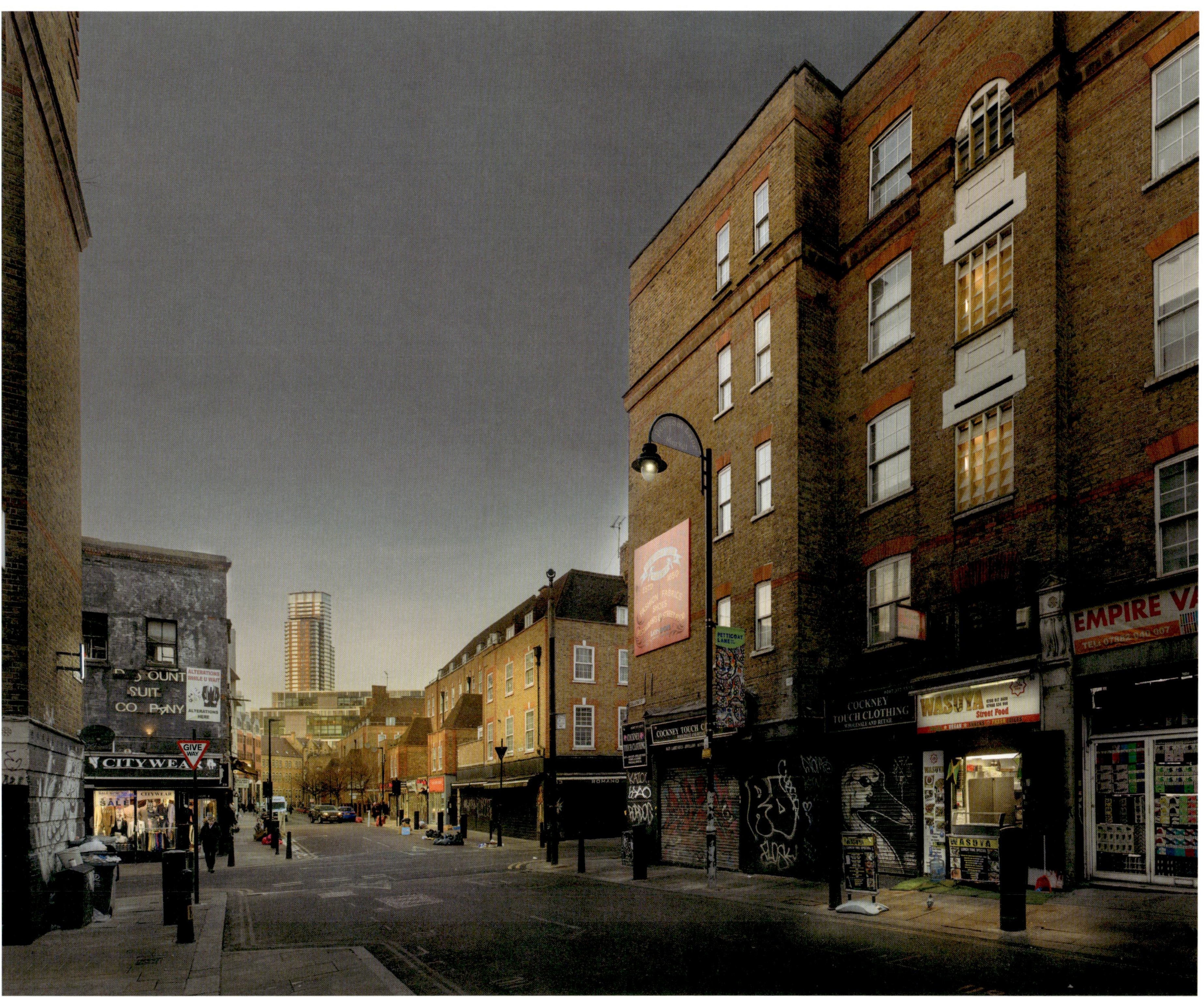
CITYWEAR
GIVE WAY
SUIT
ALTERATIONS HERE
PETTICOAT LANE
COCKNEY TOUCH CLOTHING
WHOLESALE AND RETAIL
Street Food
ROMANO

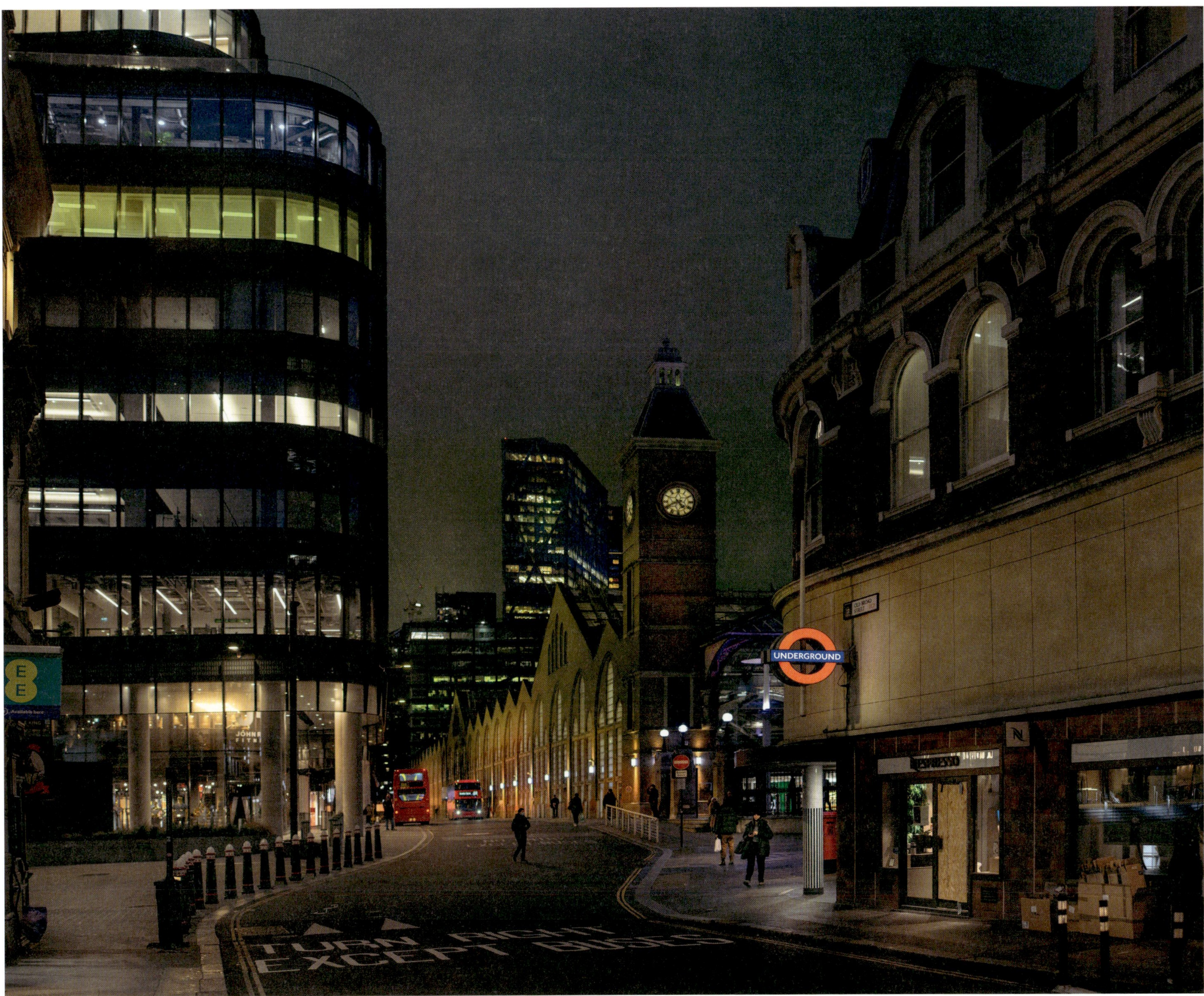
EE
UNDERGROUND
TURN RIGHT
EXCEPT BUSES

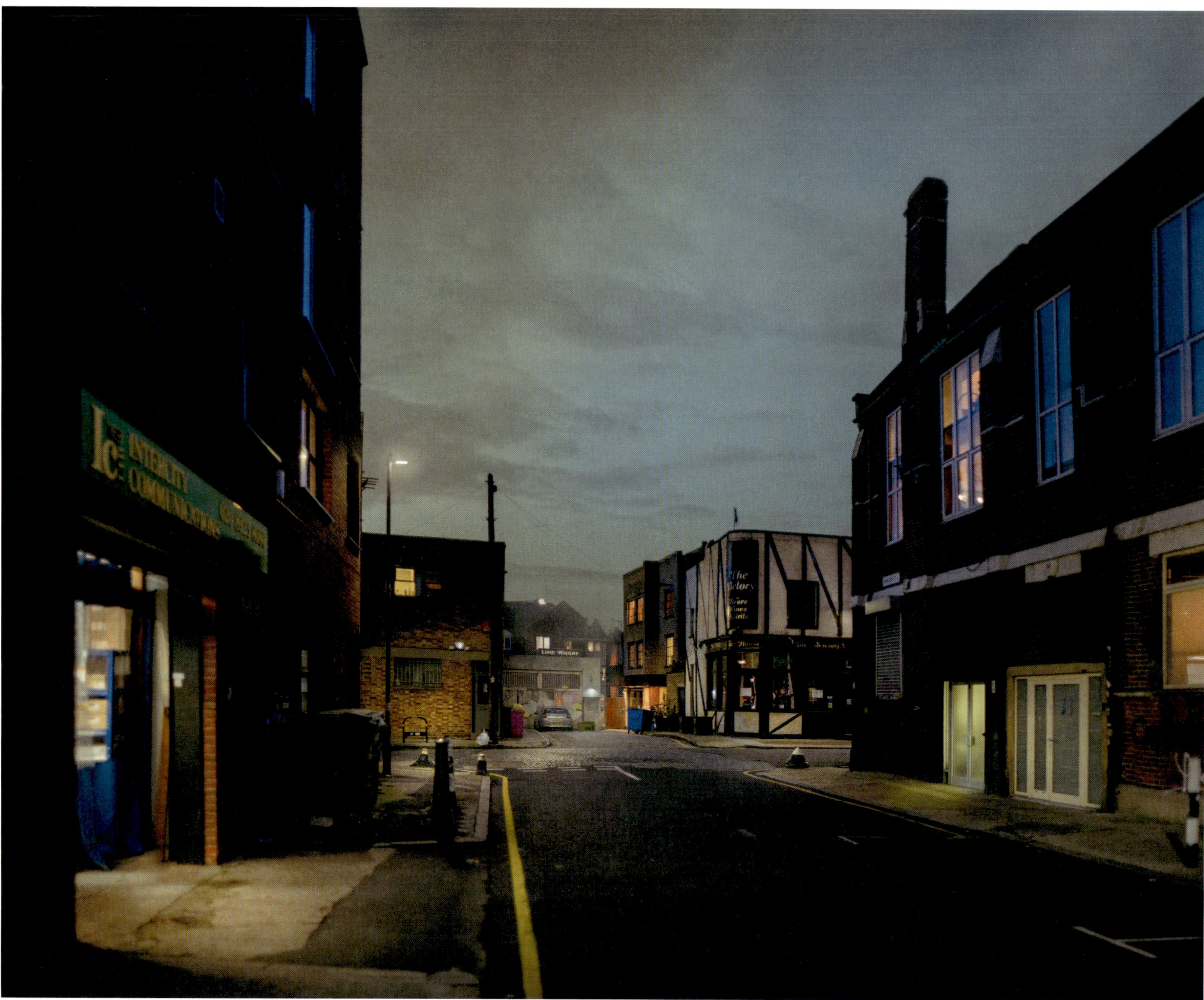
INTERCITY
COMMUNICATIONS
LIME WHARF

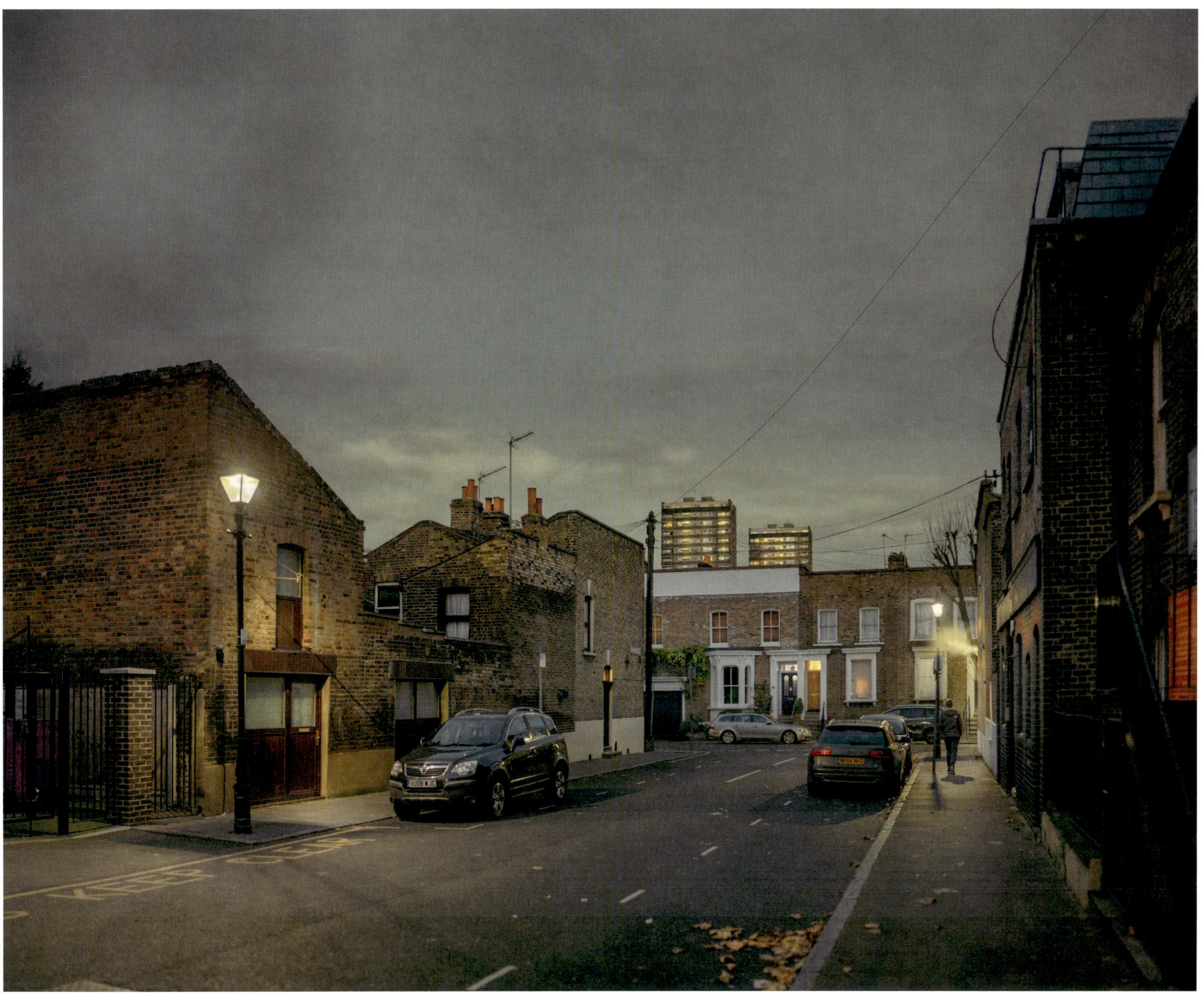
KEEP CLEAR

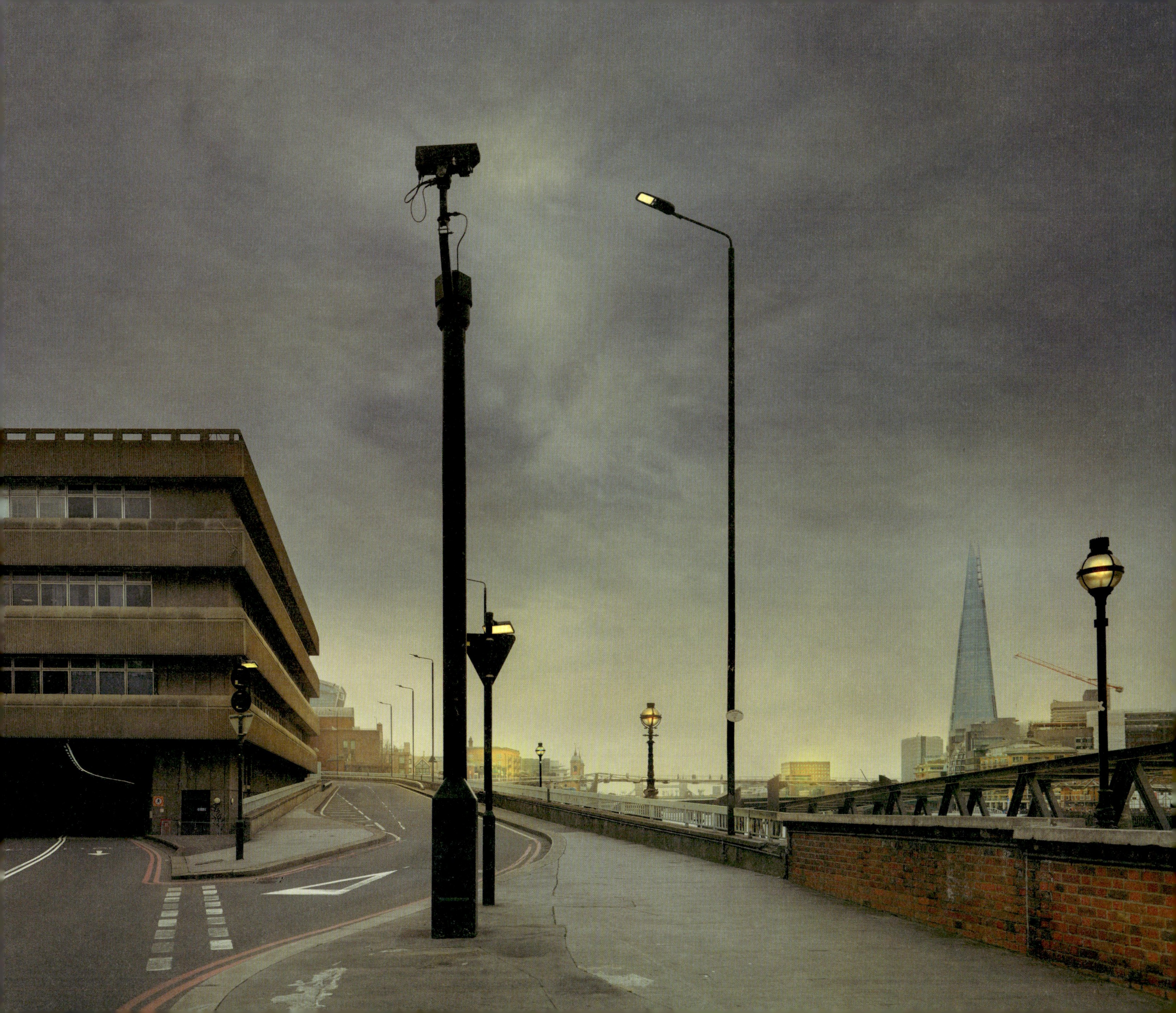

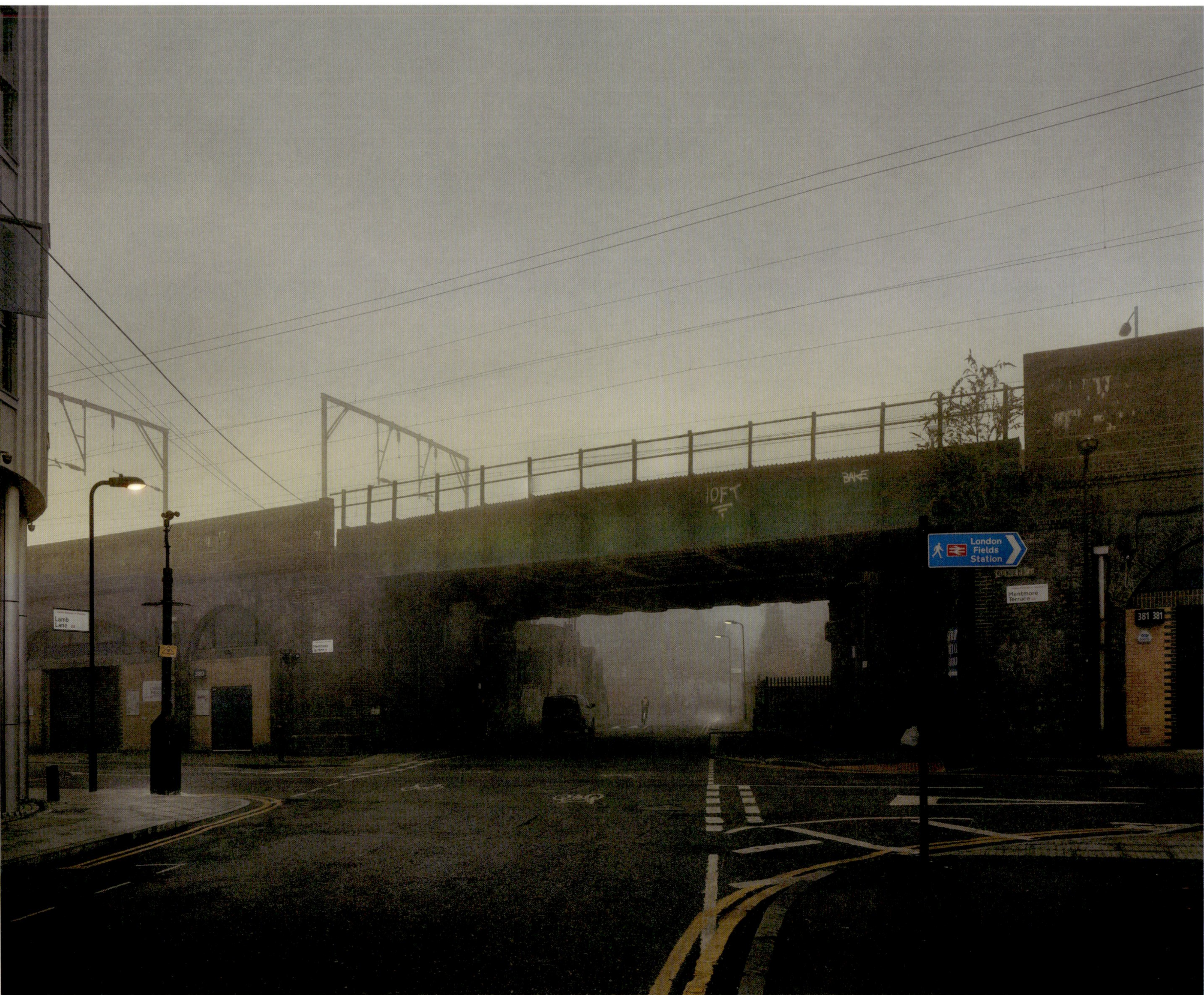

London
Fields
Station
Mentmore
Terrace
381 381
Lamb
Lane

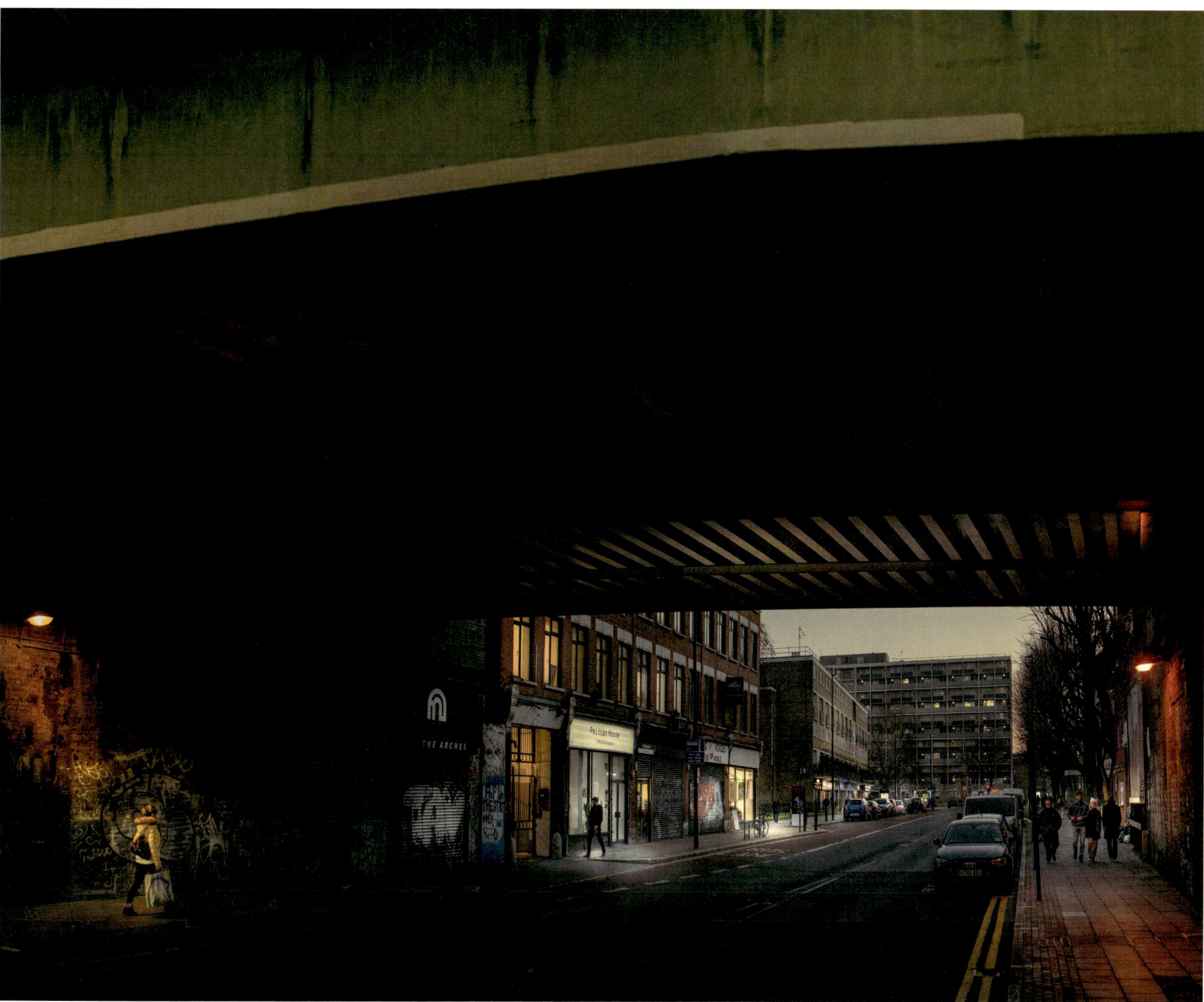
THE ARCHES
Pelican House
Cafe & Workspace

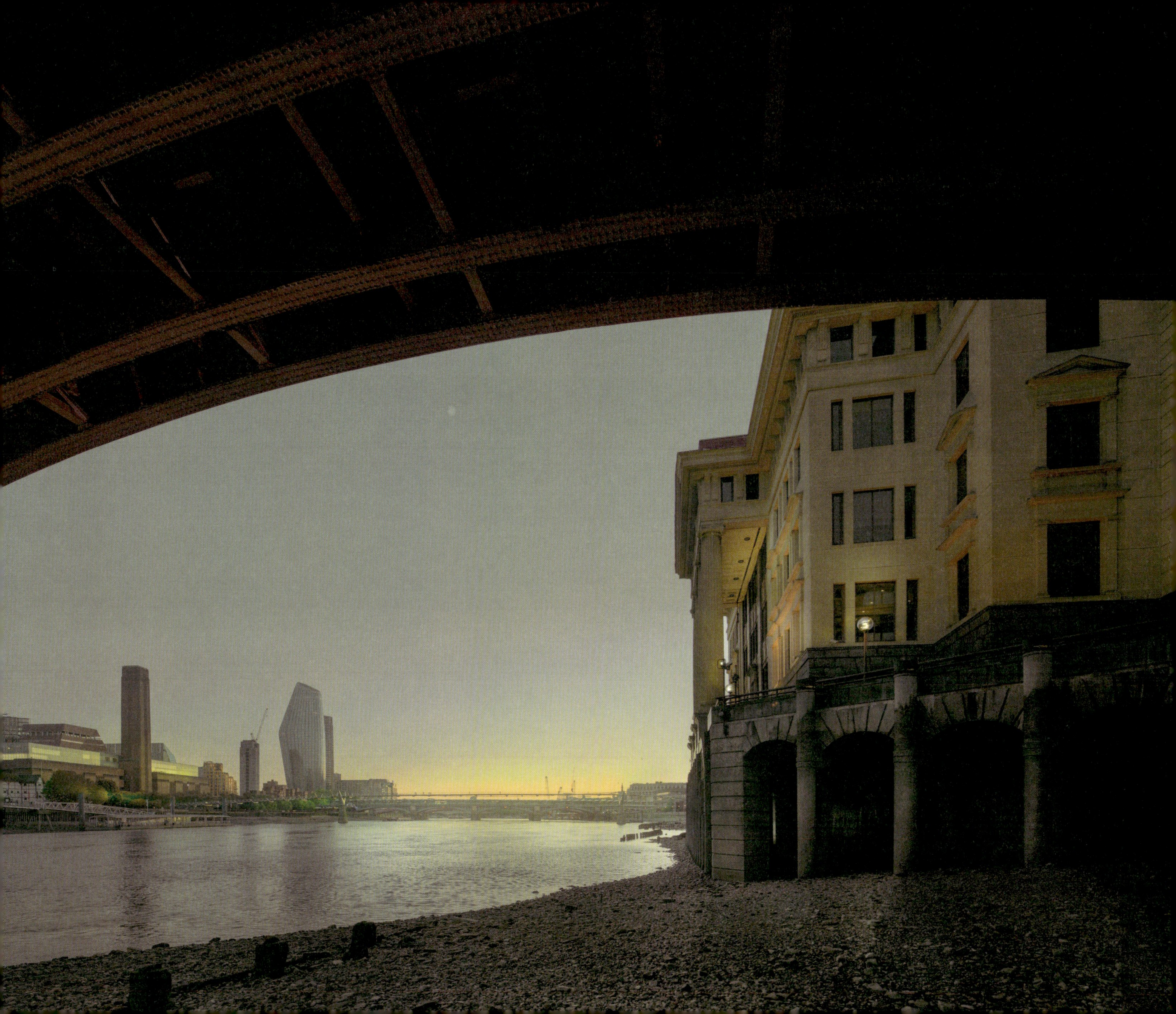

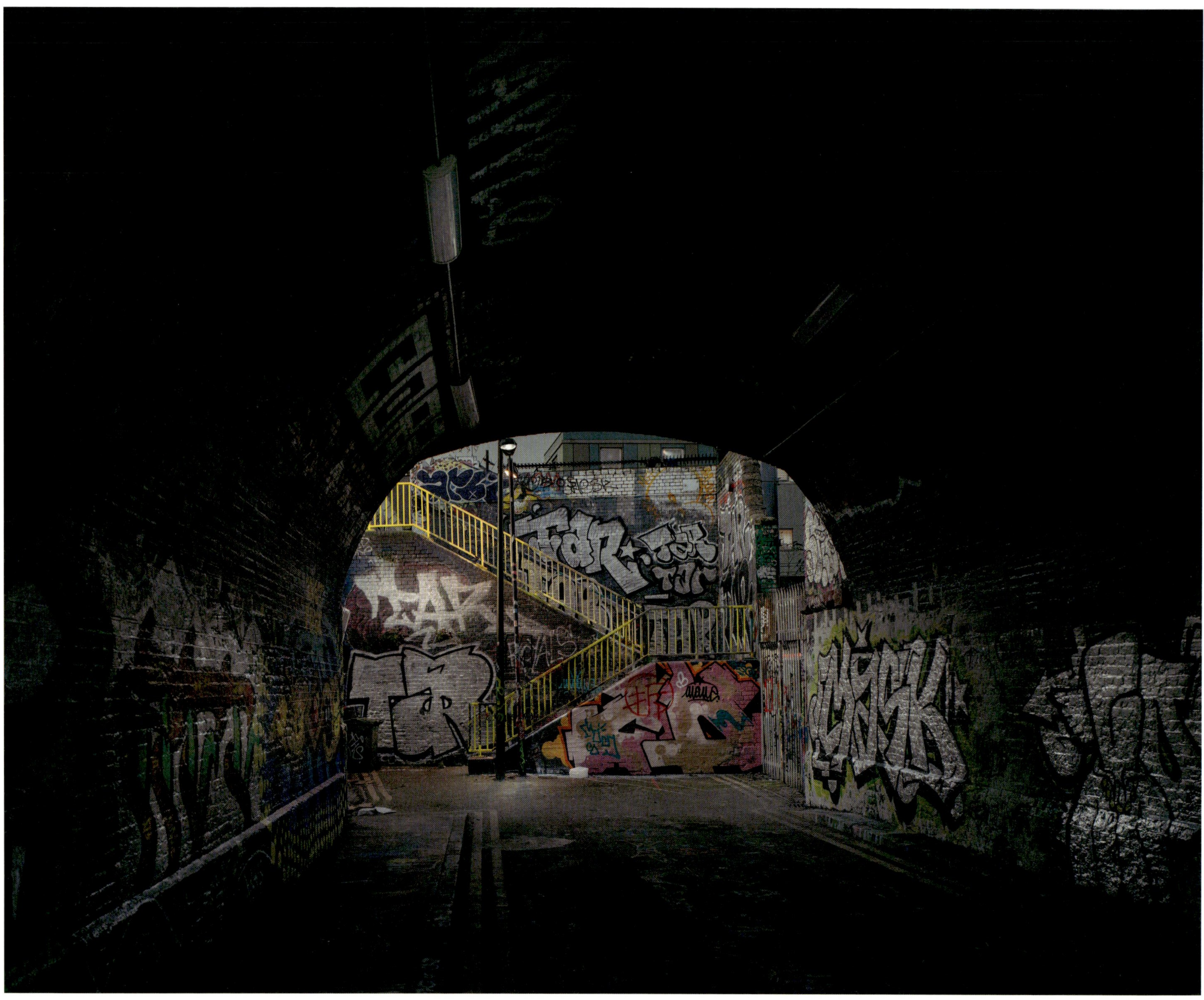

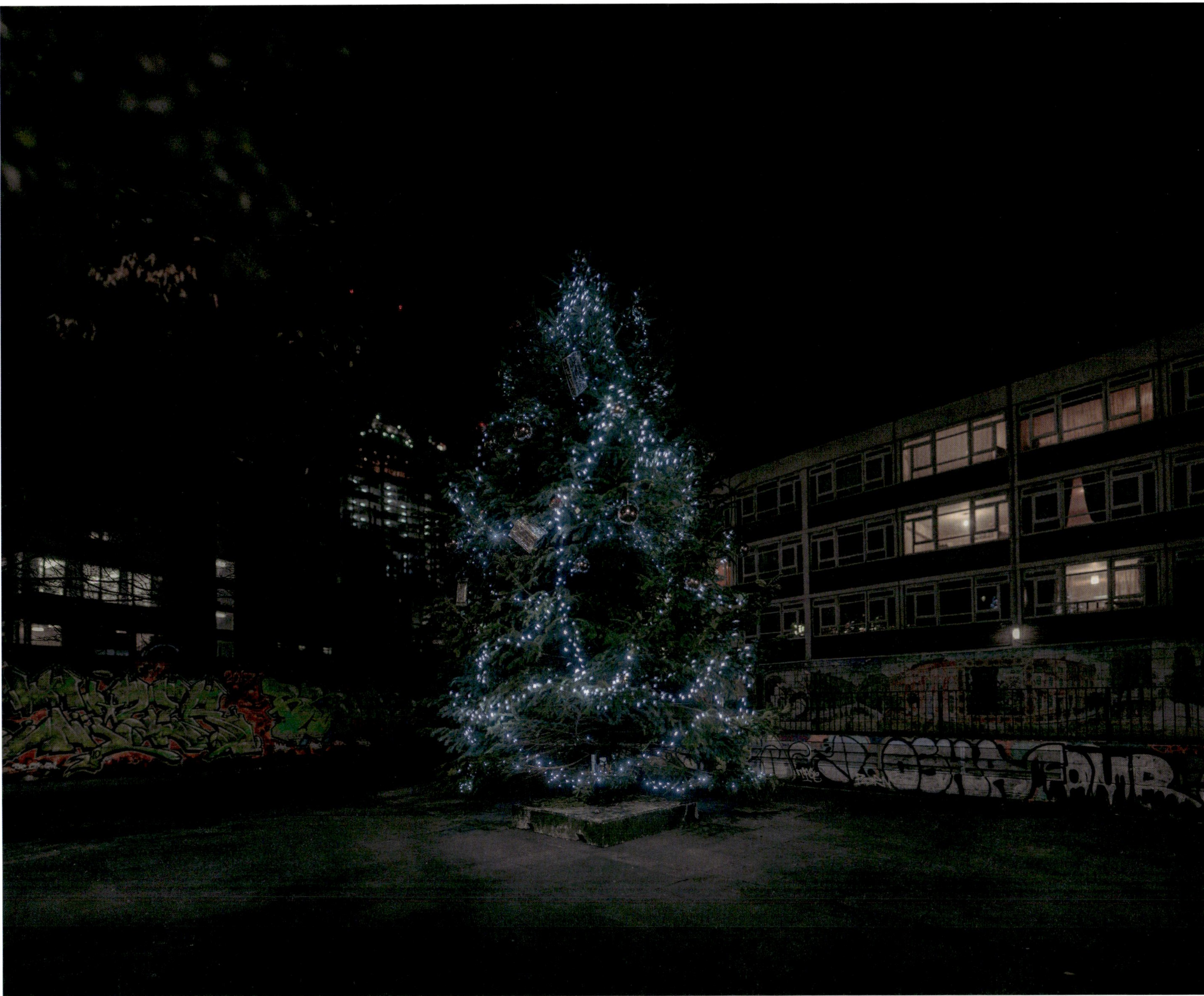

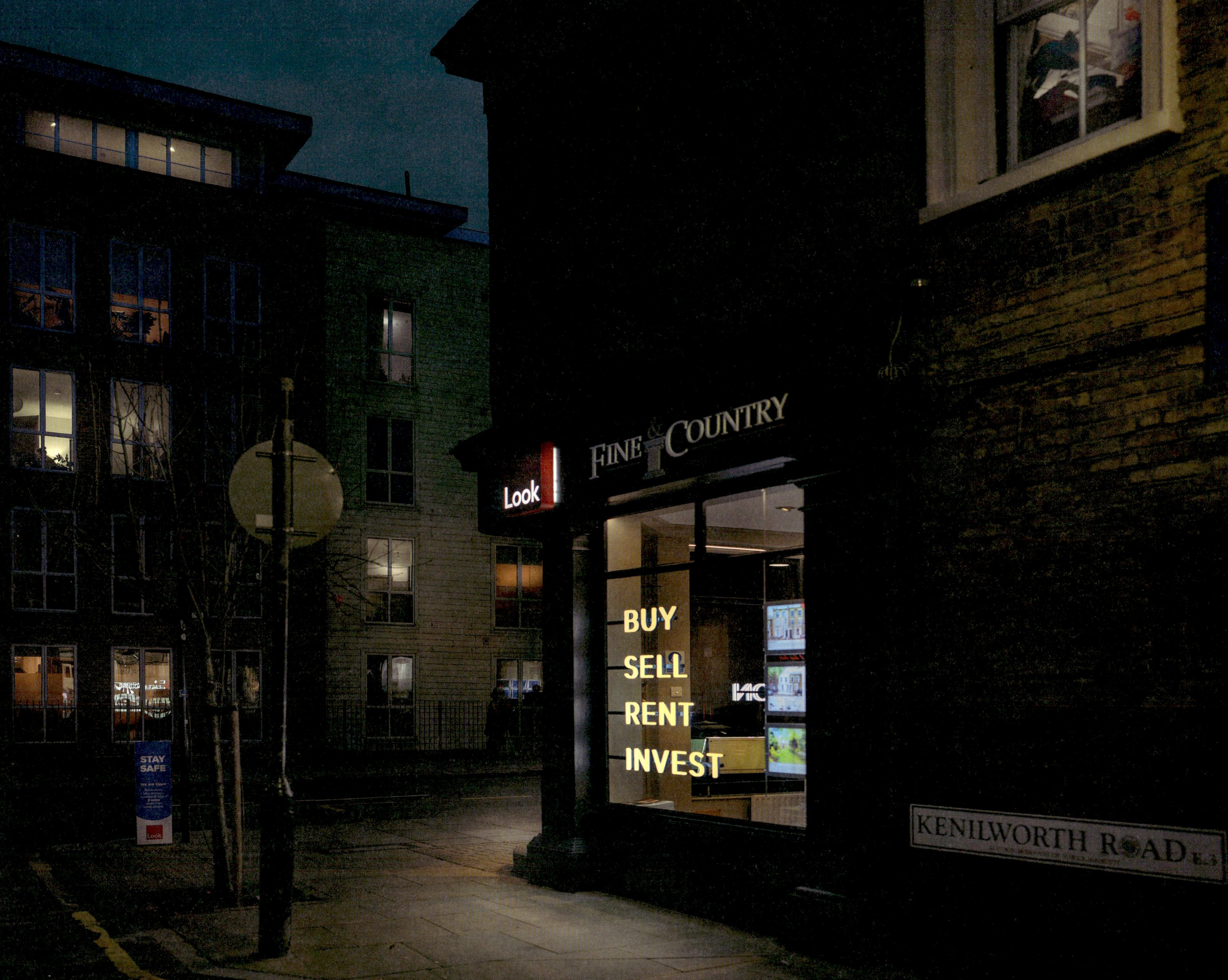
FINE & COUNTRY
Look
BUY
SELL
RENT
INVEST
STAY SAFE
KENILWORTH ROAD E.3

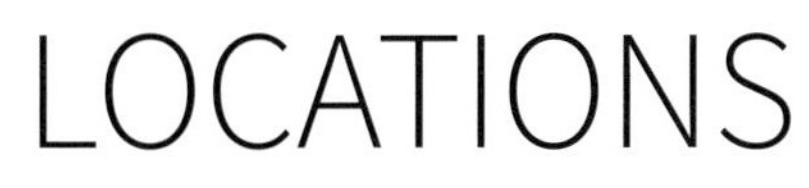
LOCATIONS

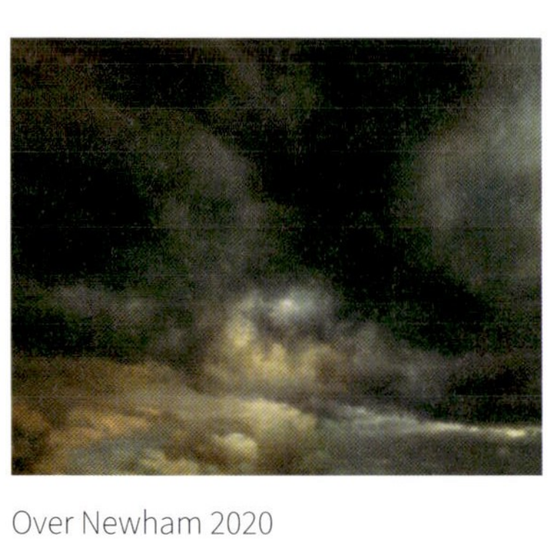
Over Newham 2020

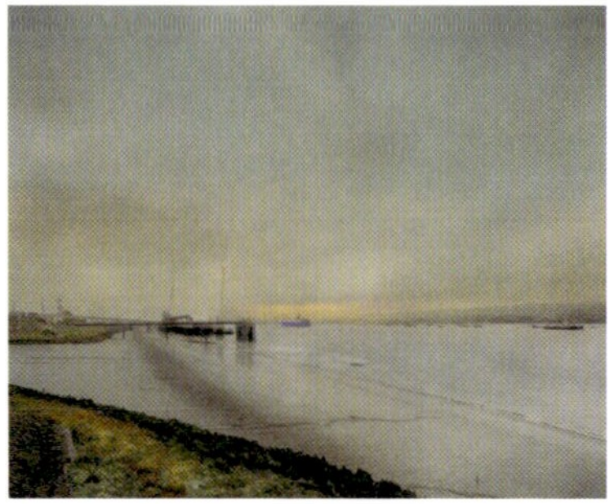
Tilbury 2019

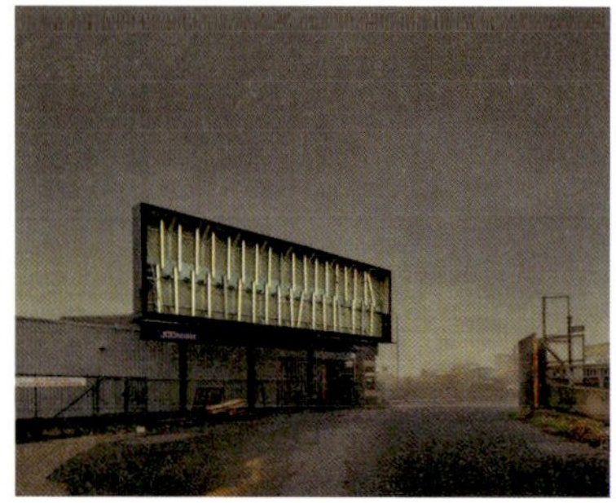
Bromley-by-Bow 2009

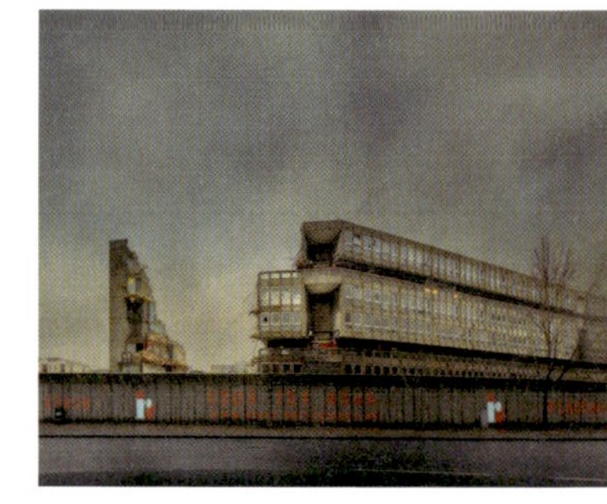
Poplar 2017

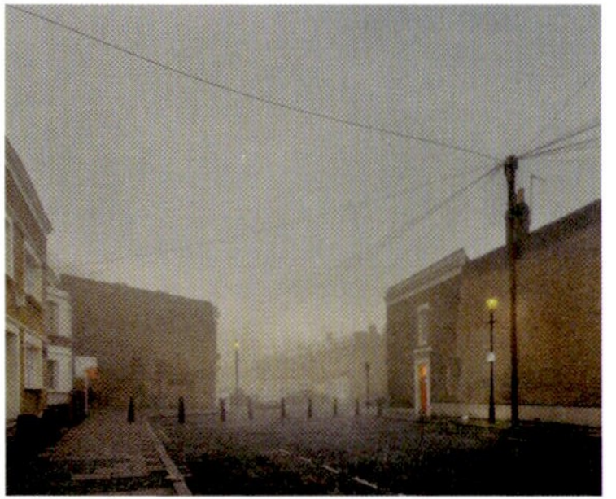
Mile End 2016

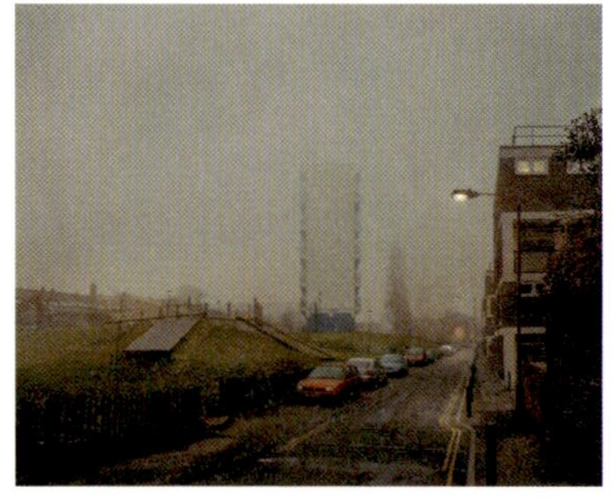
Hackney 2012

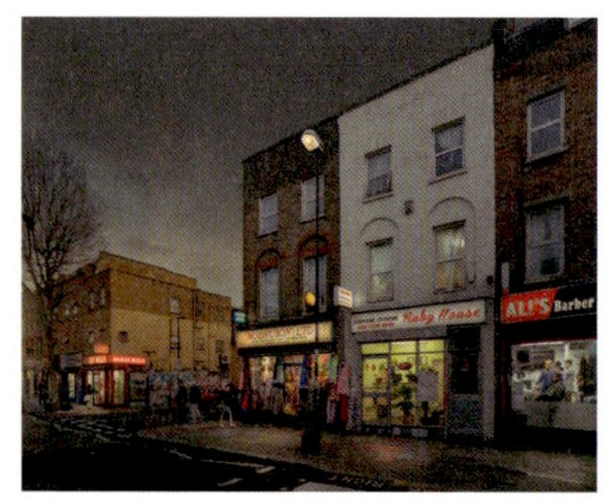

Bethnal Green 2020

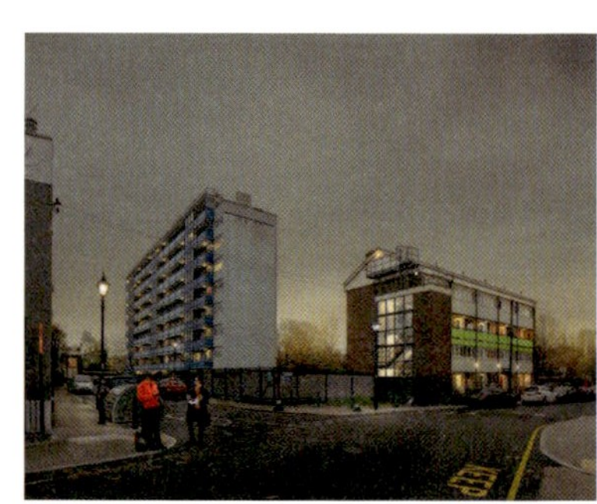
Bow 2020

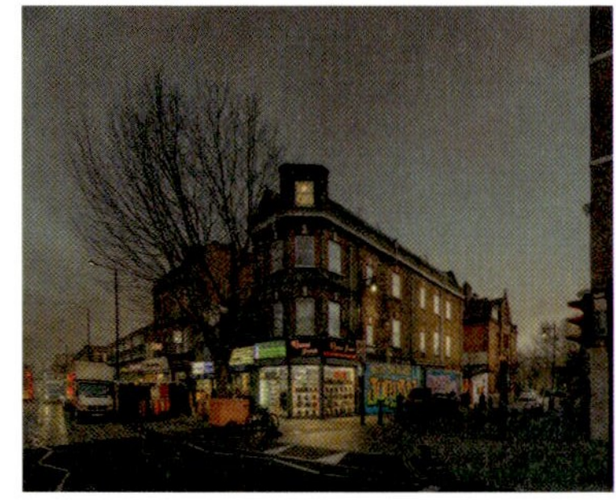
Bethnal Green 2020

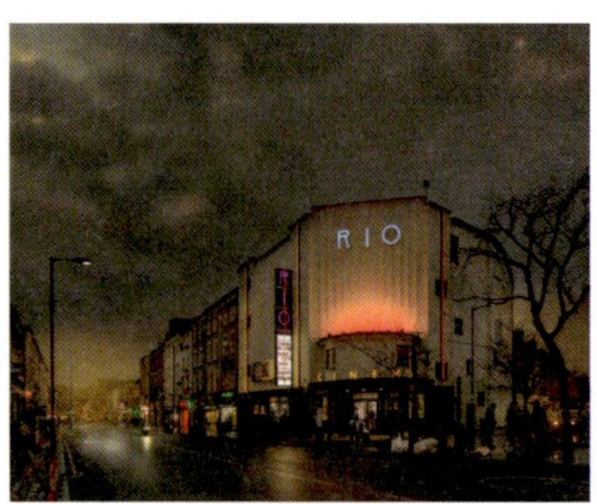

Dalston 2020

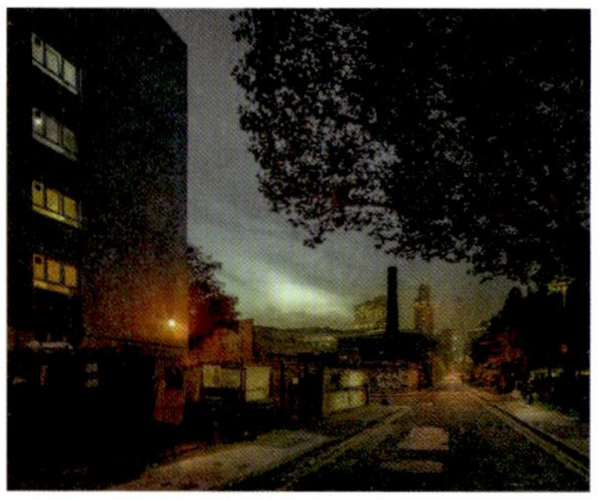
Spitalfields 2019

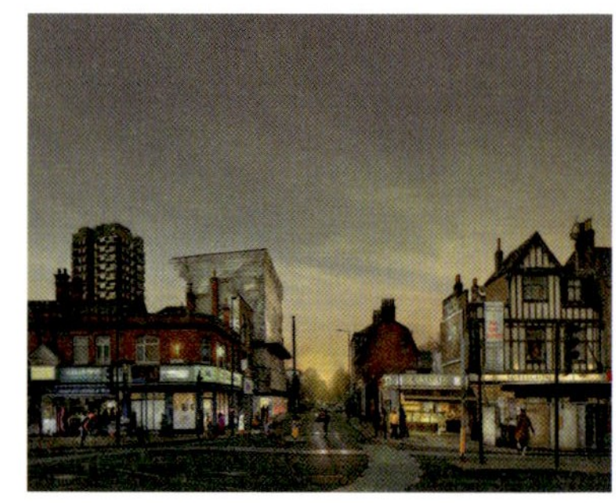
Whitechapel 2022

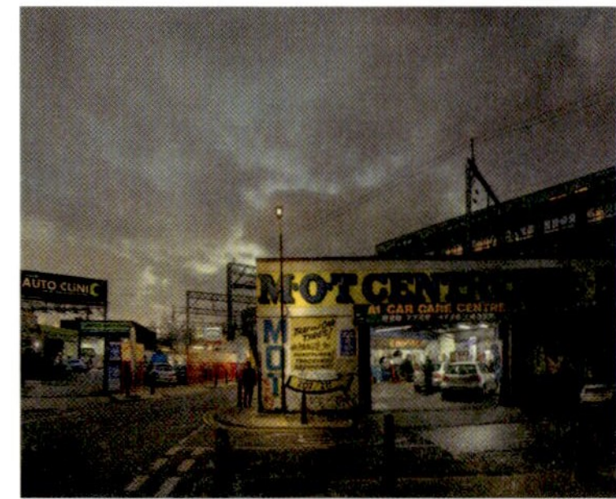

Bethnal Green 2020

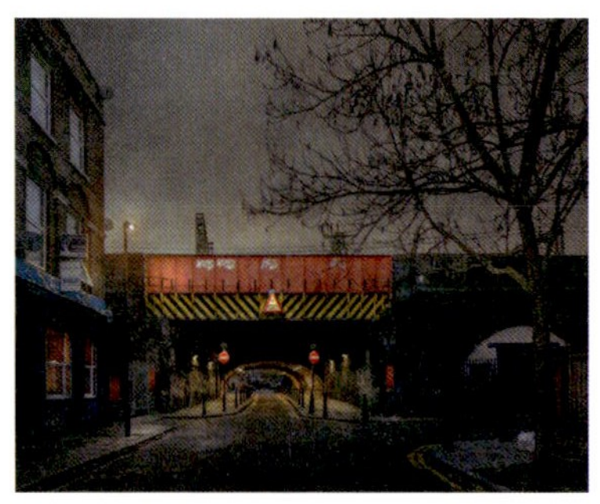
Bethnal Green 2020

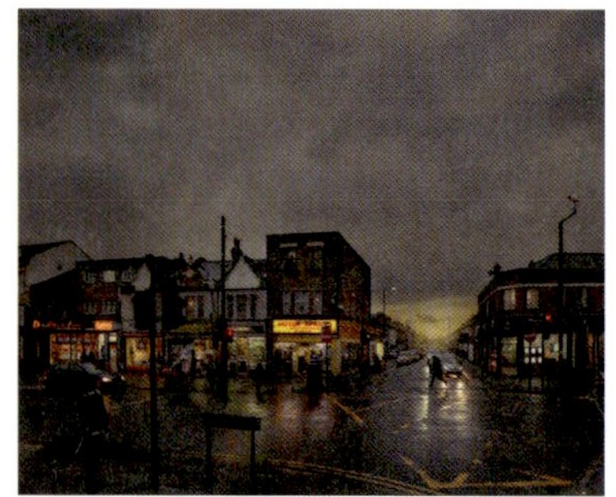
Manor Park 2019

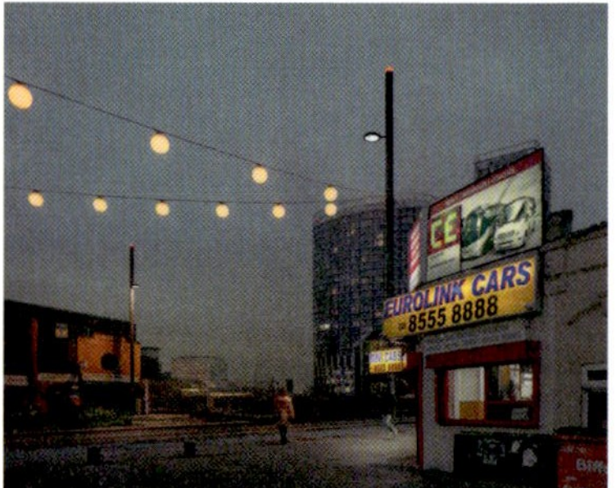

Stratford 2020

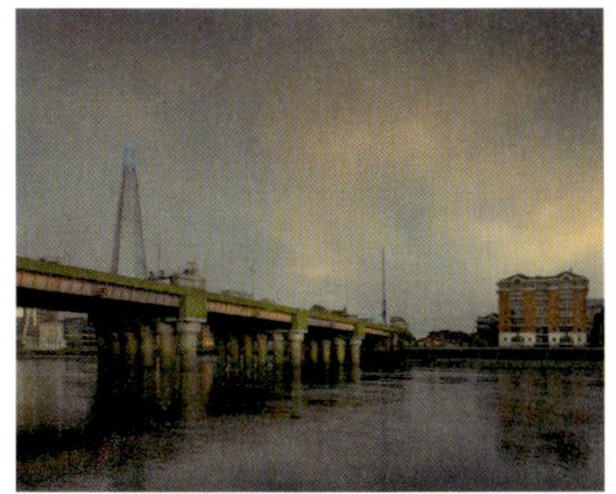
Queenhithe 2020

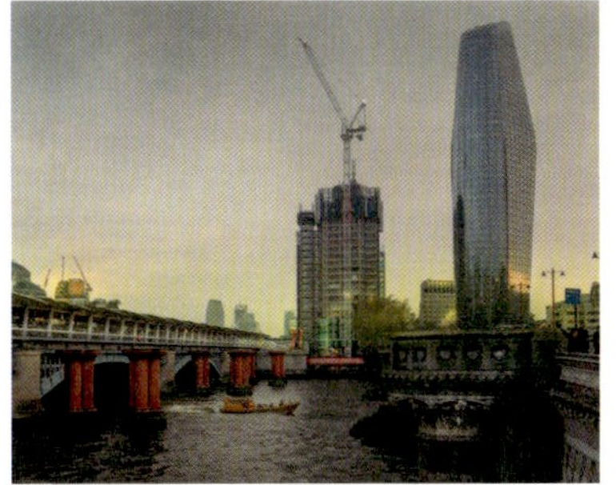
Blackfriars 2025

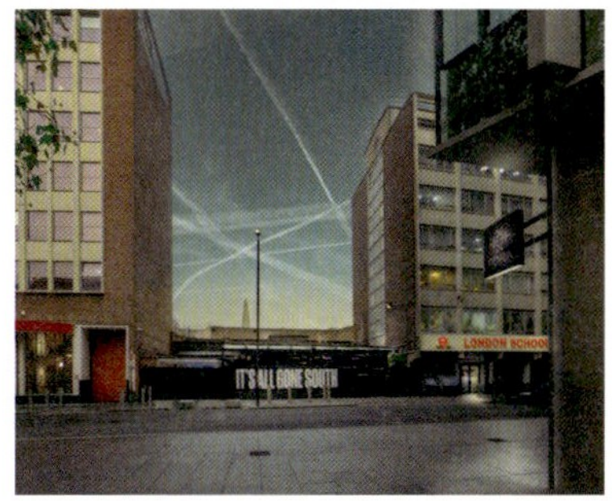
Southwark 2024

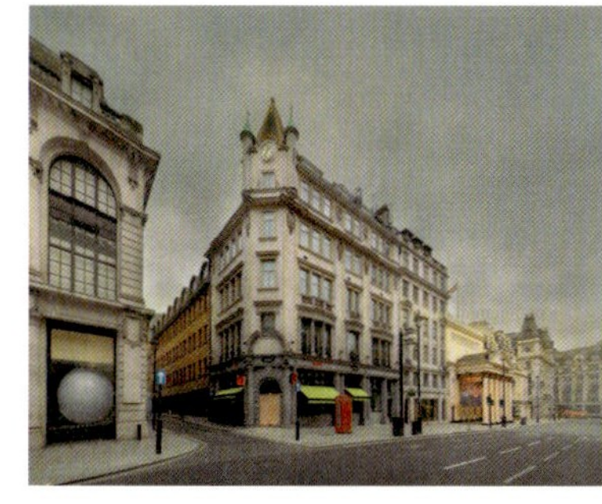
Haymarket 2020

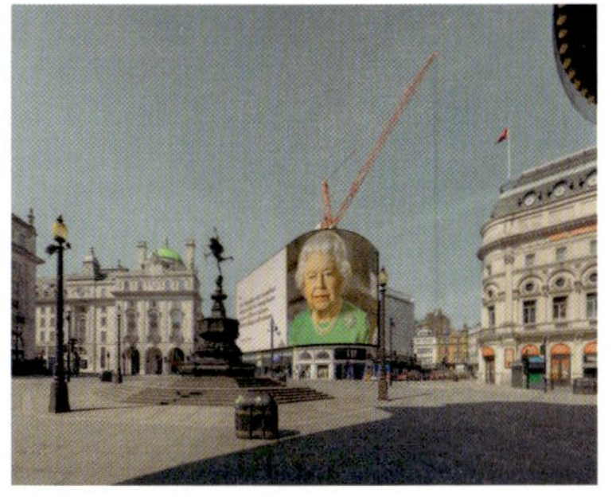
Piccadilly 2020

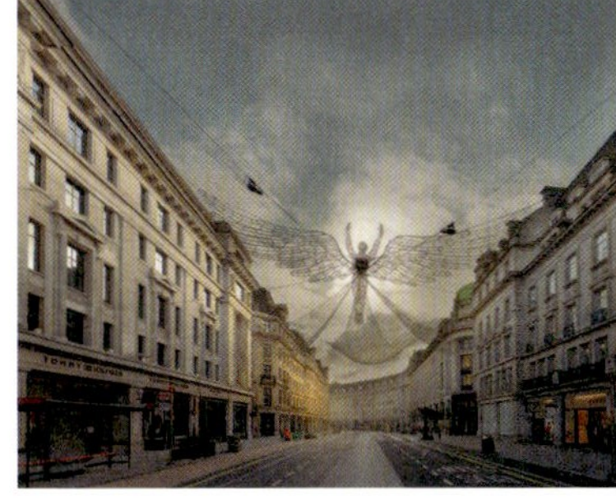
Regent Street 2021

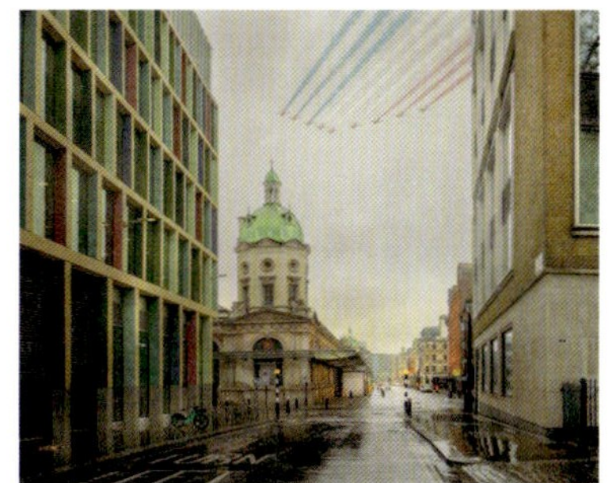
Smithfield 2023

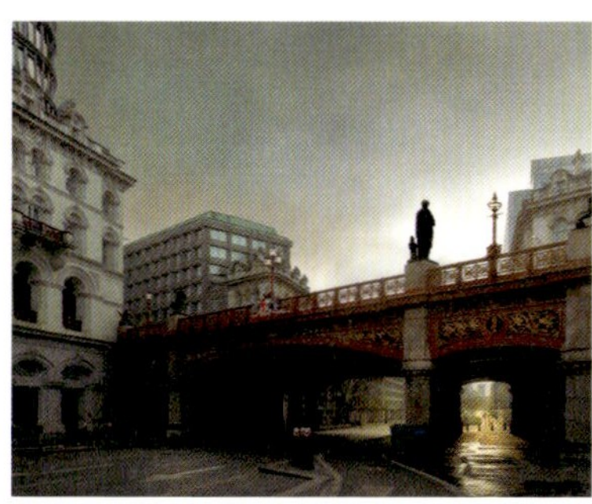
Holborn Viaduct 2021

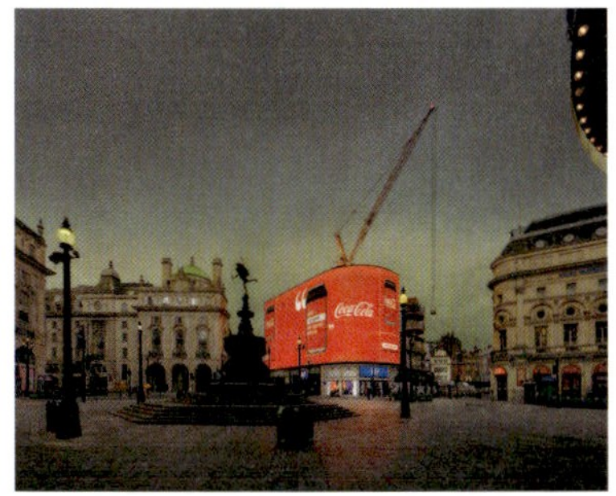
Piccadilly 2021

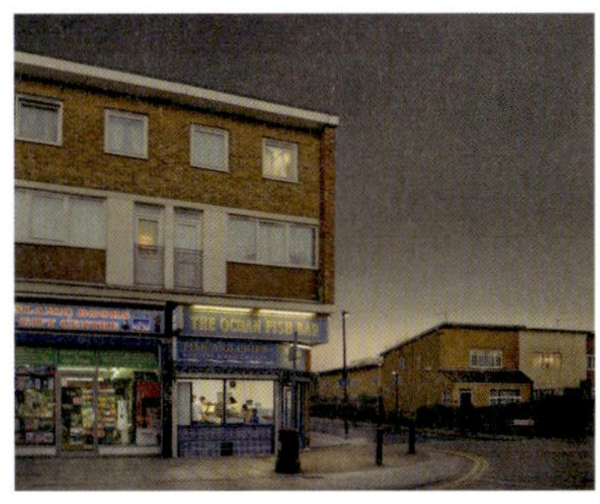
Stepney 2019

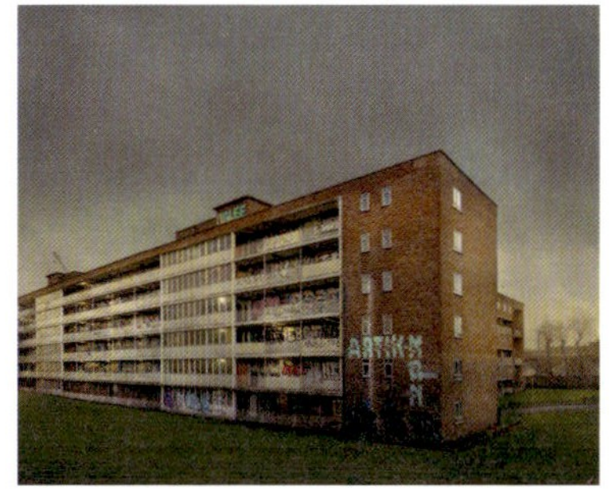
Homerton 2022

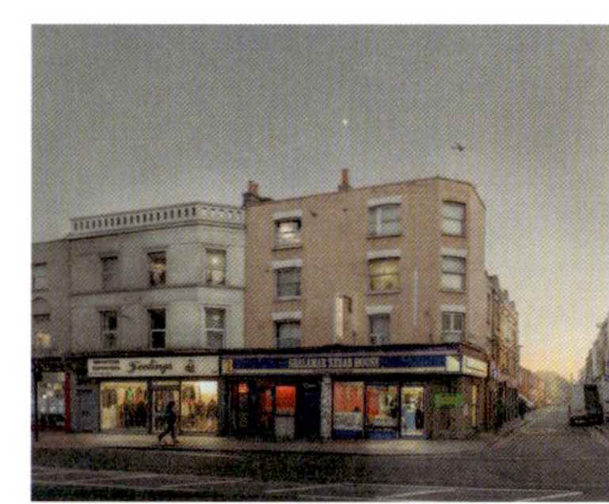
Whitechapel 2019

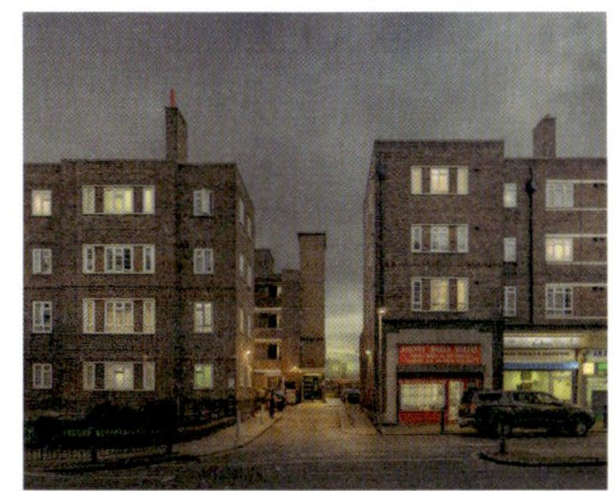
Stepney 2016

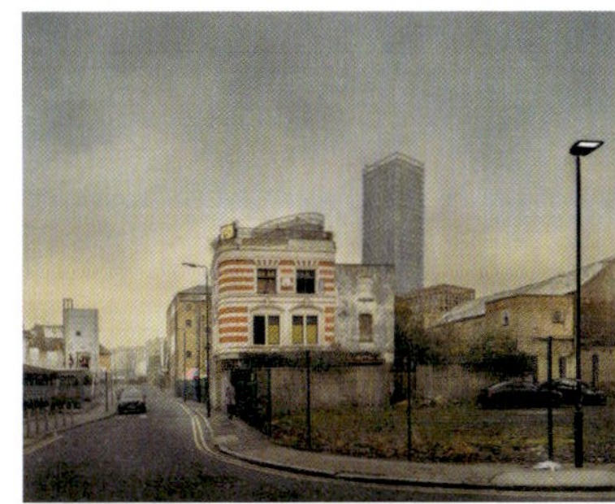
Stratford 2019

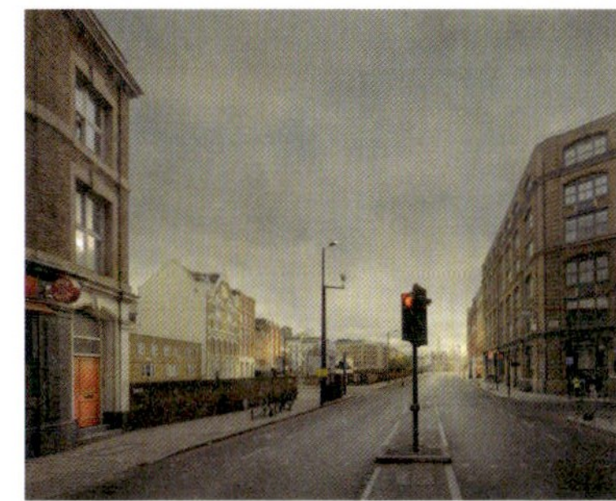
Farringdon 2021

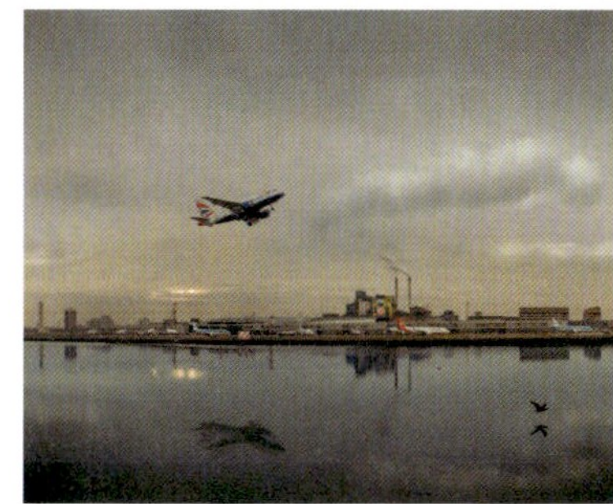
Silvertown 2019

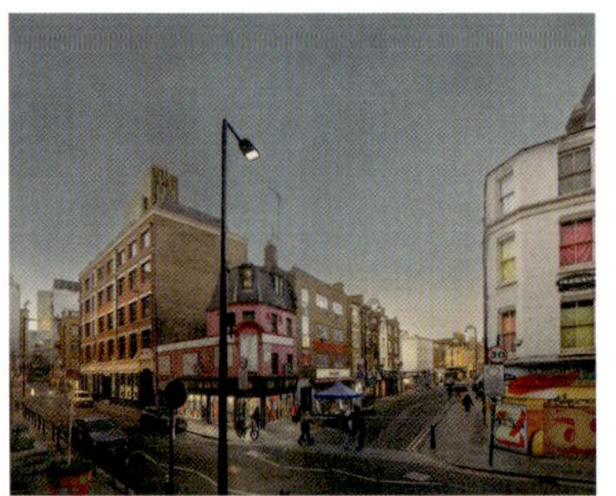
Portsoken 2023

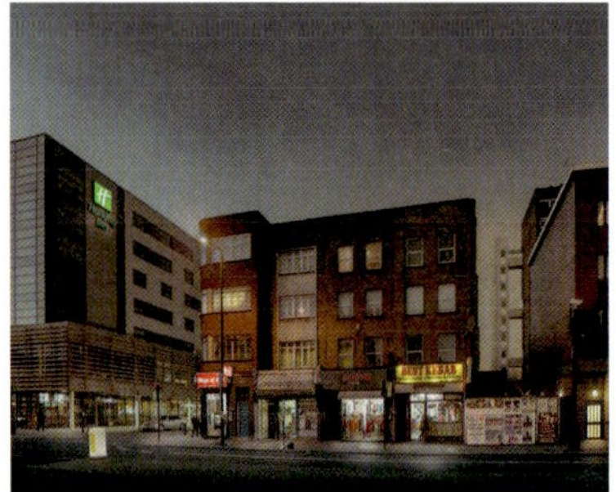
Whitechapel 2019

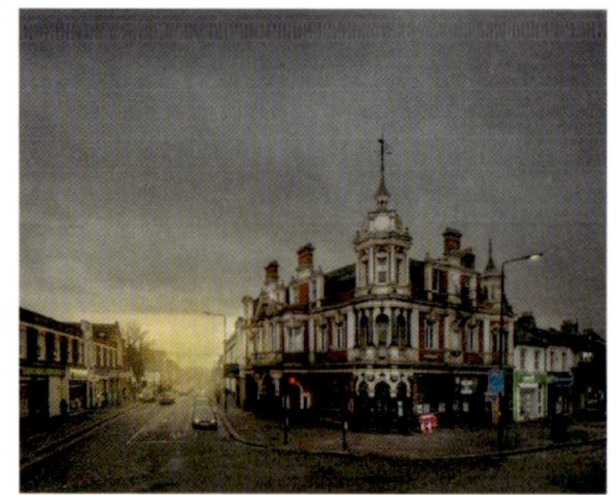
Manor Park 2019

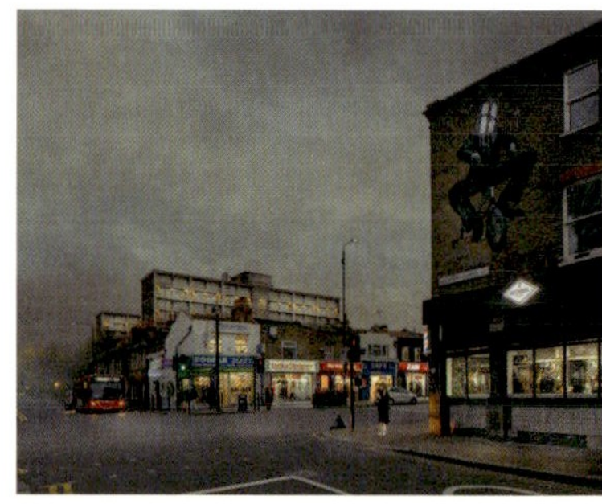
Bethnal Green 2022

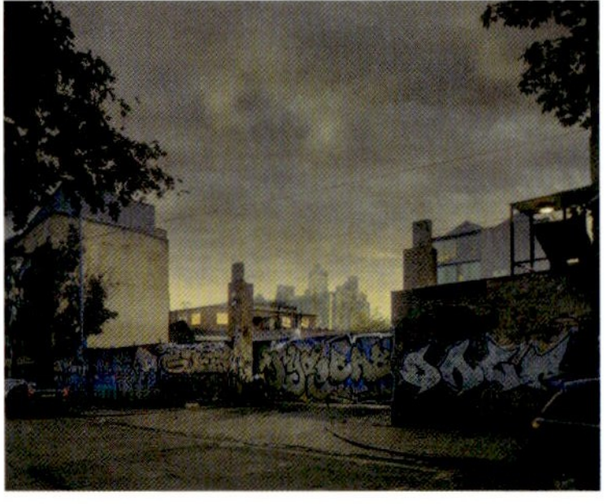
Spitalfields 2019

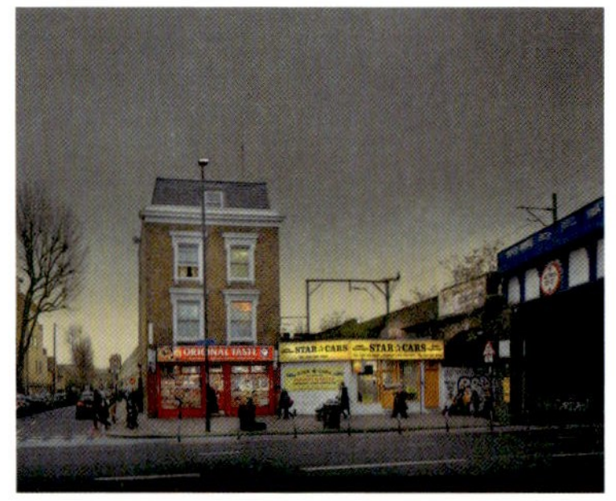
Bow 2019

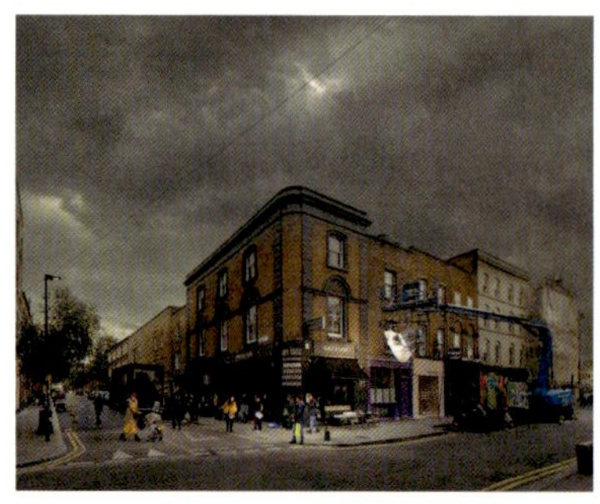
Bethnal Green 2022

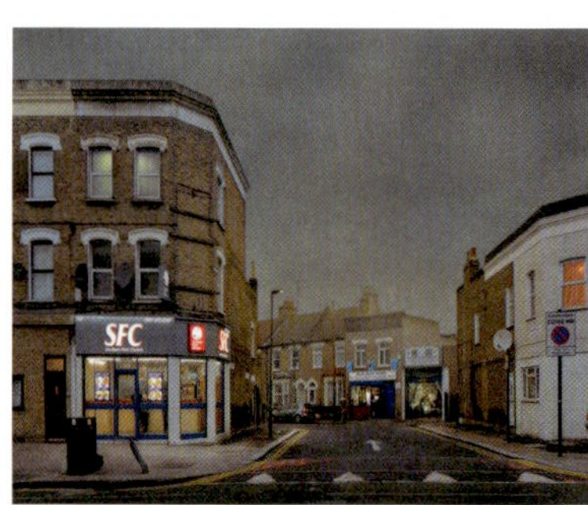

Canning Town 2019

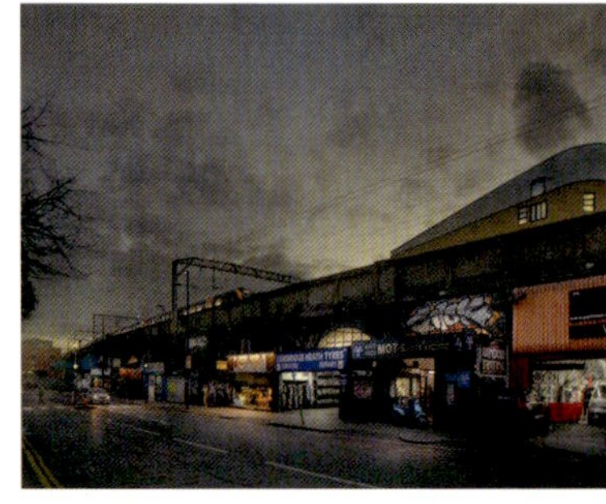
Cambridge Heath 2020

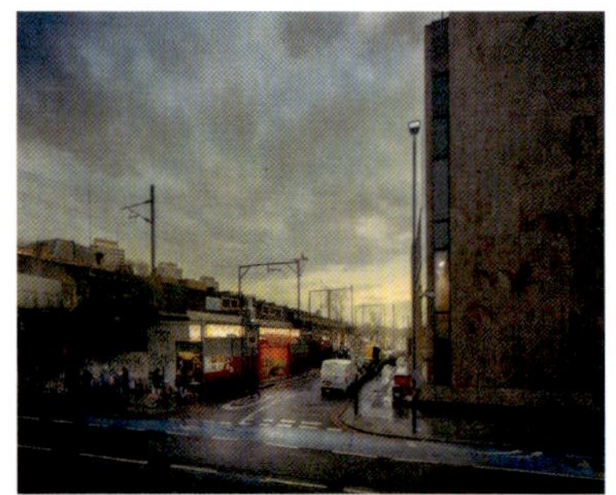
Bow 2019

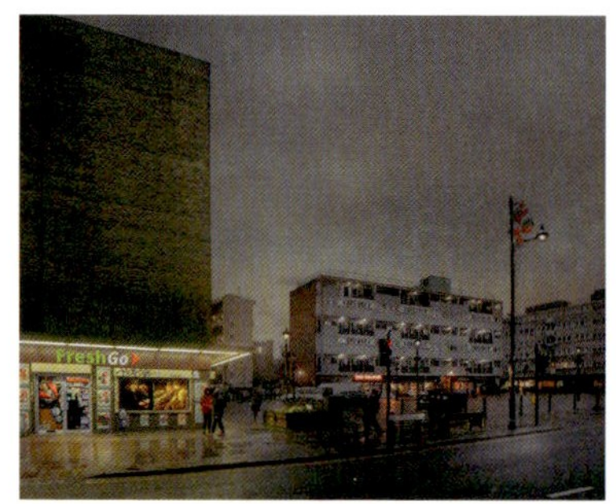

Bethnal Green 2020

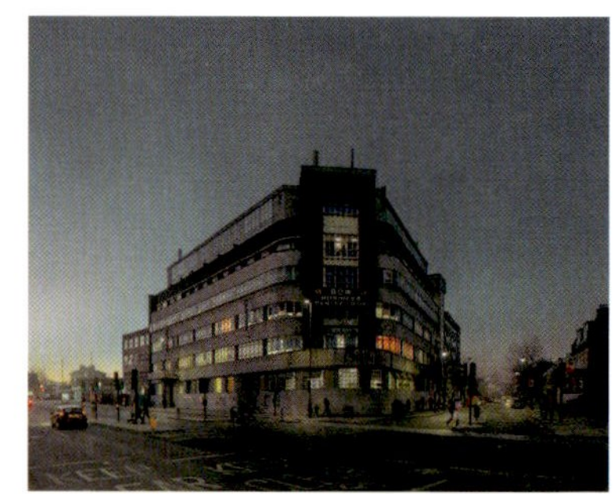
Bow 2020

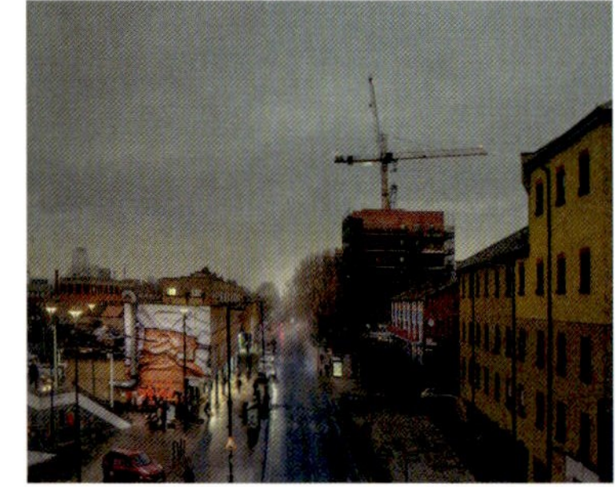
Custom House 2025

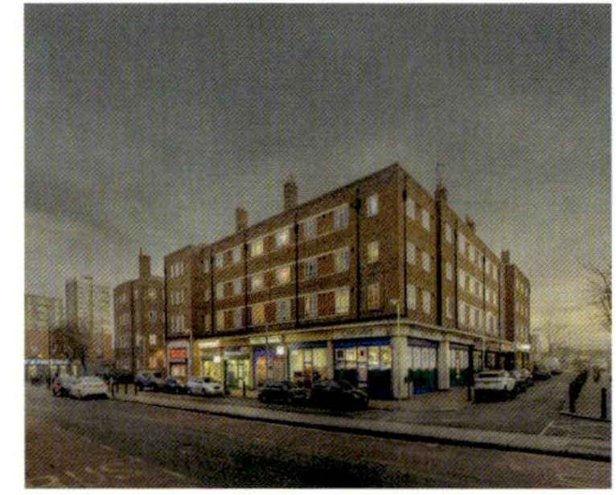
Stepney 2019

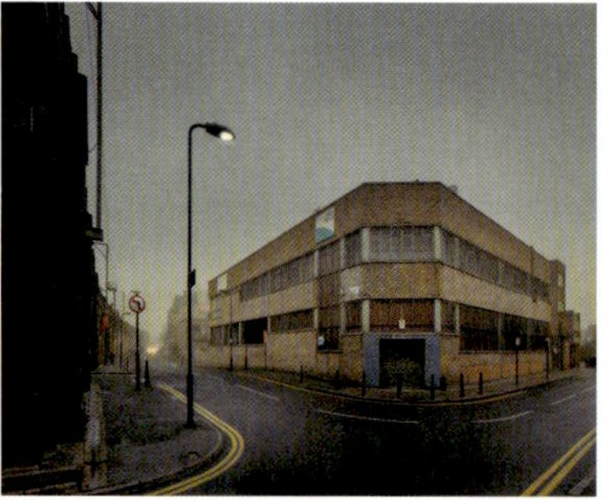
Hackney 2011

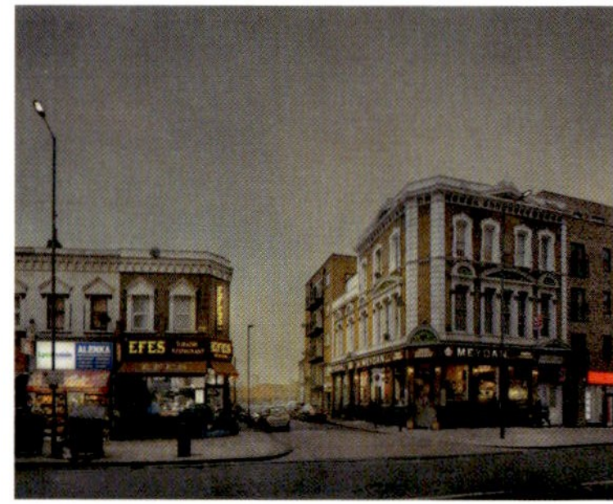
Canning Town 2019

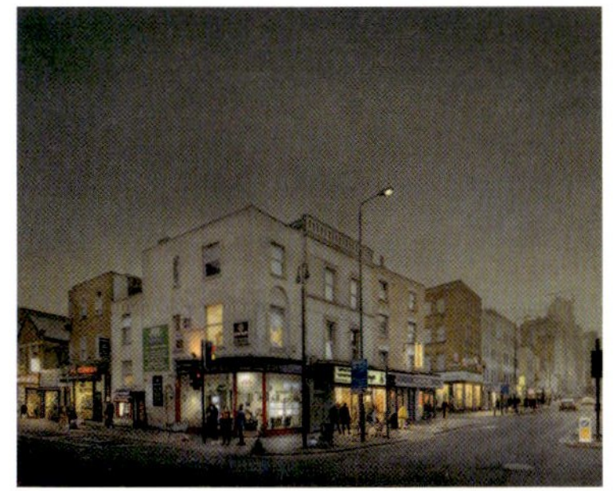
Whitechapel 2019

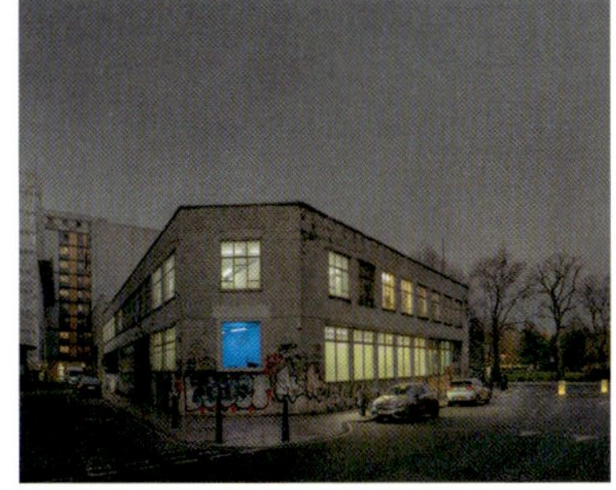
Bethnal Green 2022

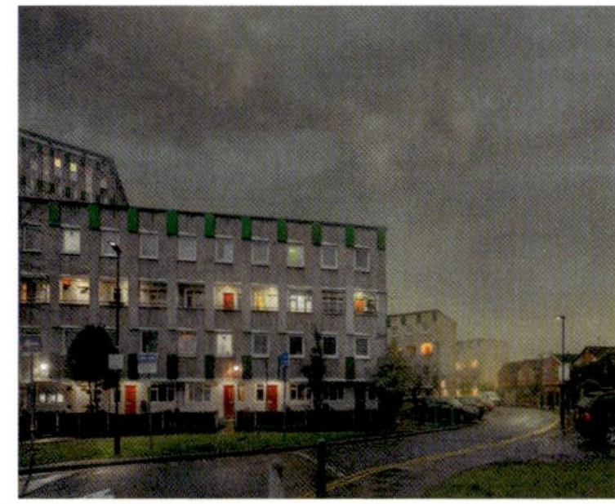
Bethnal Green 2020

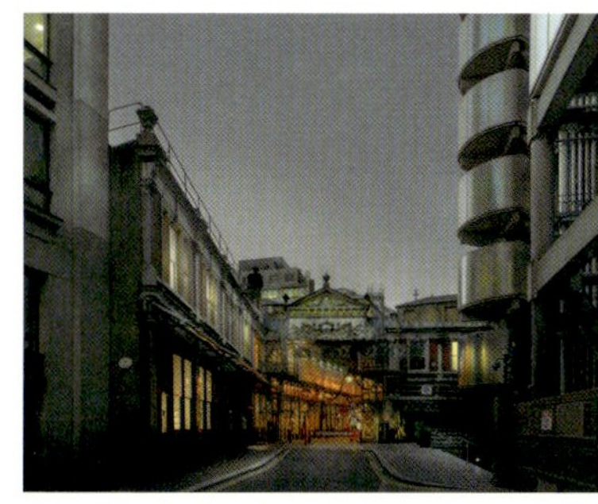
Leadenhall 2022

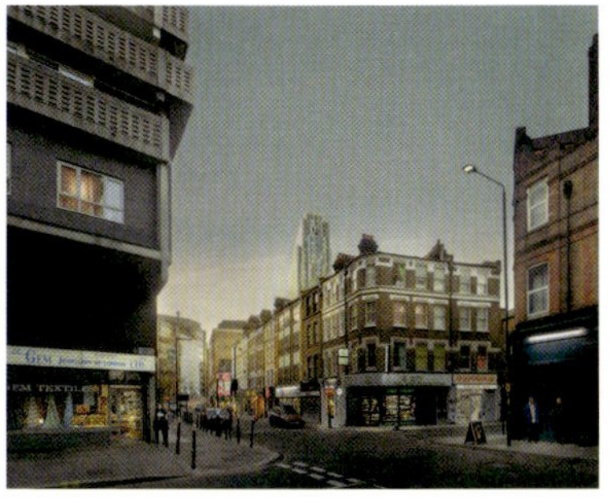
Houndsditch 2023

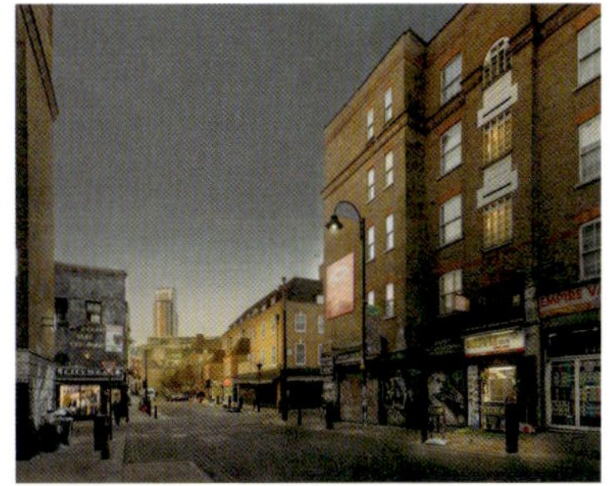
Portsoken 2023

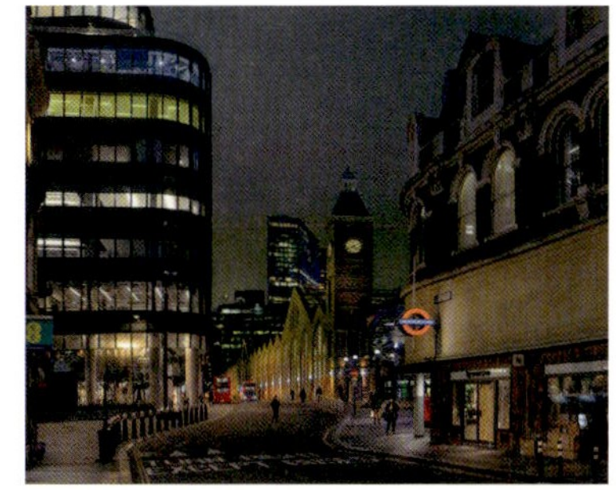
Liverpool Street 2022

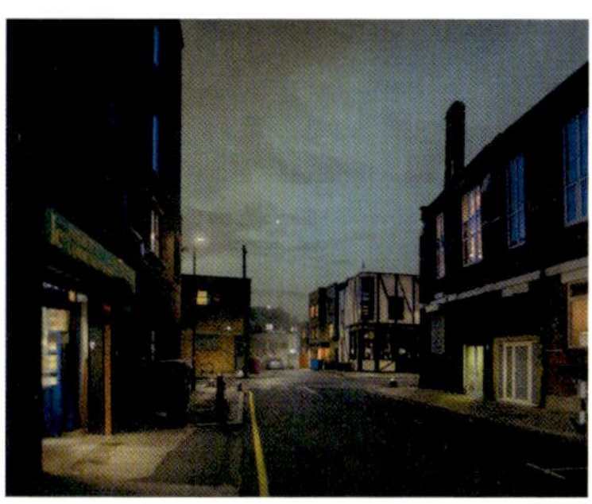
Bethnal Green 2020

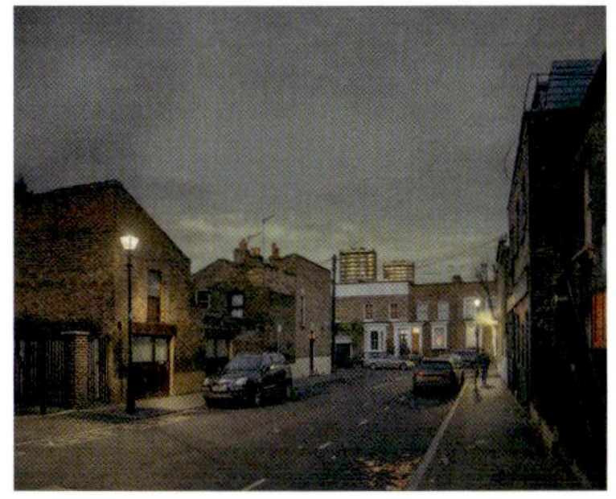
Bow 2019

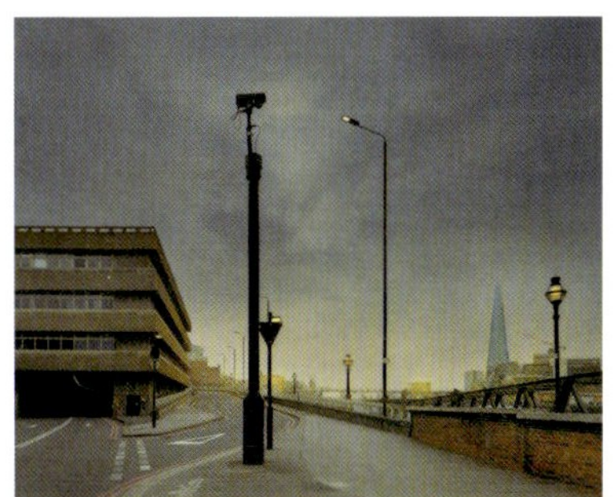
Blackfriars 2021

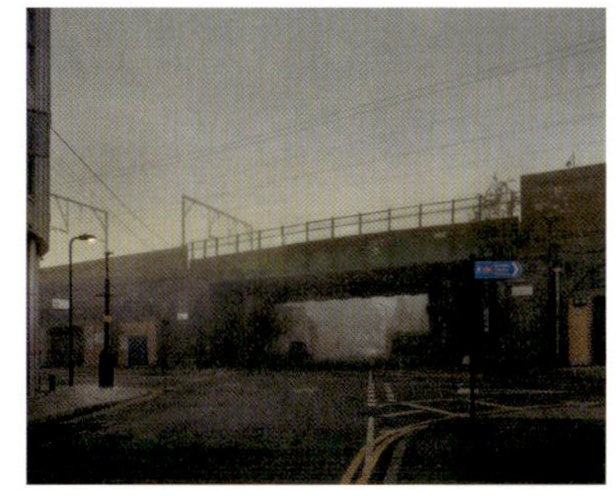
Hackney 2011

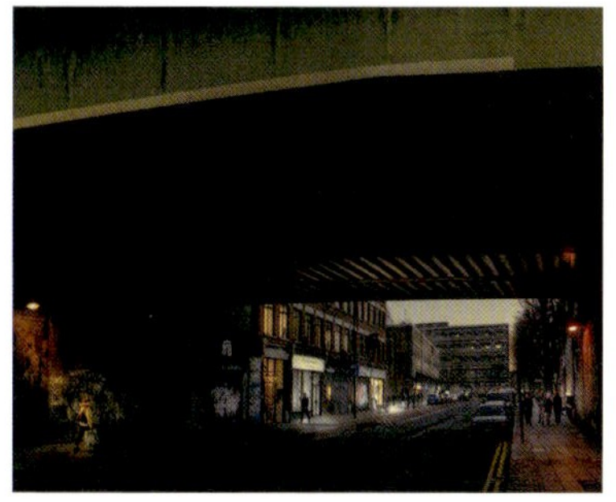
Cambridge Heath 2023

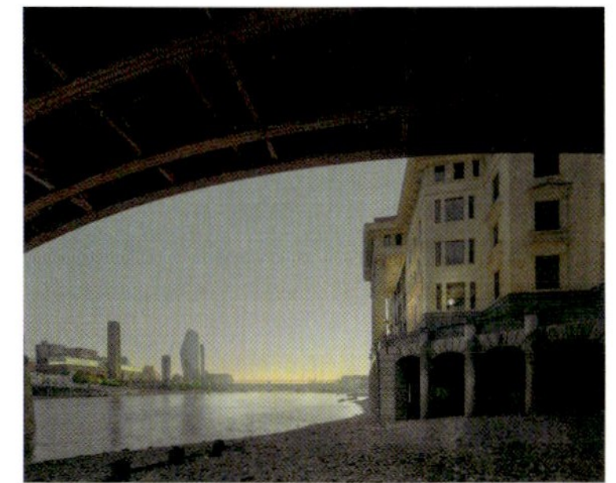
Queenhithe 2020

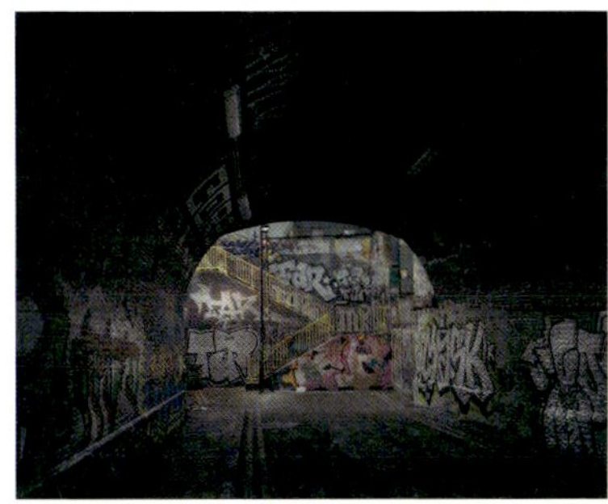
Shoreditch 2022

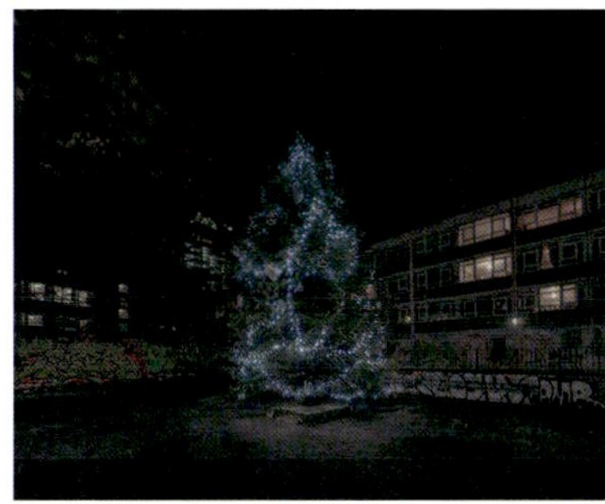
Shoreditch 2017

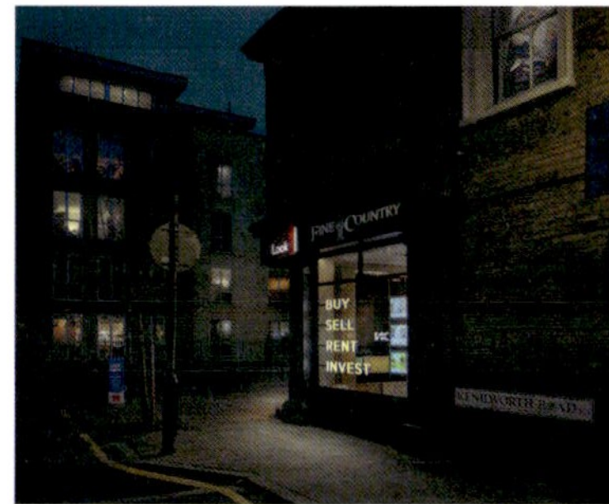
Bow 2022

The generosity of all our Kickstarter supporters is very much appreciated. In particular we would like to acknowledge the following people.

Matthew Appleton
Patricia Baker-Cassidy
Paul Bass
John Bates
Mark Lawrence Beal
Julian Bester
Dawoud Bey
Karin Borghouts
Jem Dorley-Brown
Neil Burgess
Stephen Burnett
Joe Cano
Manuel Casal
Mike Chisholm
Berris Conolly
Oliver Creasy
Robert Cribbin
Raphaël Crochet
Alex Currie
Laurie Elks
Felix Glauner
Jim Gottlieb
Mike Grover
Rosie Hallam
Fabienne Hanotaux
John Hartley
David Hawley
Jepke Van Hengst
Tom Hostler
Mark Hurrell
Janet Delaney Jetton
William Iuliano
David Kregenow
Martin Larnach
Herve Laroche
Barry Lewis
David Littler
Chengwang Liu
Harriet Logan
Roy Lonergan
Patrick Marti
Neil Martinson
Peter Massingham
Kristian Mau
Jan McKenzie
Jürgen Michael
Seán Murray
Padmapani Muzquiz
Anil Mull
John Myers
Mark Nassar
Johanna Neurath
Adam Newman
Ramon Niemiec
David O'Connor
David Oliver
Mark O'Neill
Albert Carter Phillips
Mark A Phillips
Nigel Power
Faraz Ravi
Antonio Ros
Michael Ross
Kelly Rossi
Dana Rudinger
Avneet Seehra
Jonathan Self
Kenton Simons
Adam Smith
Andy Spain
Juanita Spooner
Mahesh Srinivas
David St.Clair
Barry Stewart
Mark Taylor
Sara Terry
David Thornton
Lance Tilley
Alain Wais
Tom Westbury
James Yorston

First published in the UK in 2025 by

Dewi Lewis Publishing
8, Broomfield Road
Heaton Moor
Stockport SK4 4ND
England

www.dewilewis.com

ISBN: 978-1-916915-18-3

Design and Edit: Dewi Lewis
Print: EBS, Verona, Italy

Chris Dorley-Brown
www.modrex.com